SHP FINANCIAL

I'm a Financial Scatterbrain

A look at the world of retirement planning through the eyes of a reformed scatterbrain

CHUCK NILOSEK

Copyright © 2013 Chuck Nilosek
All rights reserved.
ISBN: 1480284203
ISBN 13: 9781480284203

Table of Contents

Preface 5

Chapter One: To Succeed at Old Age, You Have To Start Young 13

Chapter Two: Make Planning Number One on Your To-Do List 19

Chapter Three: Why You Must Plan for a Specific Income 29

Chapter Four: The Truth about Tax-Deferred Savings Plans 35

Chapter Five: Building a Case for Tax-Free Income 39

Chapter Six: Young People: Do What You Love, Love What You Do 43

Chapter Seven: What Would I Tell Myself If I Could Write a Letter to Me? 47

Chapter Eight: You Don't Need a New Year to Make a Resolution! 53

Chapter Nine: Seniors, Understand Your Health Options 59

Chapter Ten: Who Should Consider a Reverse Mortgage? 63

Chapter Eleven: Why There May Be a Financial Pot of Gold for Those Who Can Think Outside the Box 69

Chapter Twelve: How Do We Protect Our Most Valuable Assets? 73

Chapter Thirteen: Paying Our Fair Share of Taxes Doesn't Mean Paying More 79

Chapter Fourteen: It's Time to Start Putting the "Us" Back in "the USA" 83

Chapter Fifteen: Open Letter to the President 89

Chapter Sixteen: Control What You Can; Accept What You Can't Control 95

Chapter Seventeen: Clearing the Air about Annuities 99

Chapter Eighteen: To Win at Planning, You Have tTo Vanquish Human Nature 109

Chapter Nineteen: Some Things That Glitter Just May Be Gold 117

Chapter Twenty: When You See Bias in the Media,
Follow the Money Trail 121

Chapter Twenty One: Avoiding the Specter of Final Expense 125

Chapter Twenty Two: Preparing for Turbulent Times Ahead................131

Chapter Twenty Three: Braving a Snowstorm to
Solve an Estate Problem 135

Acknowledgments

No matter the project, if it turns out to be successful, there are many people to thank and praise. If you think this book is a horrific mess, then these are the people I want you to blame! However, I hope that you find it to be funny, interesting, informative, thought-provoking, and meaningful.

First on my list of important people are all of my teachers from grade school on. Without their help and guidance, this book would have remained a dream, a collection of incomplete thoughts and regrets in my cluttered brain. These amazing people were always patient, encouraging, and inspirational. High school introduced me to Gerry Golden (who, by the way, chose this year, of all years, to call it quits. I think he was waiting for one of his successful pupils to finally thank him in a major publication). He led me to the beauty and wonder of our United States. I instantly became a lifetime addict of the National Park System, due to his passion. When I write, I often try to cultivate a message that resonates with people who might live in the plains of Texas and the mountains of Utah. I recognize and appreciate the diversity of thought that exists all over our great country. The American spirit courses through my veins, and that is because of him.

My message of thanks goes out to every single teacher I ever had over the years. Even the bad teachers taught me lessons I hold dear today. Not all people are easy to work with—yet, that is how life works. The workplace and world are filled with difficult people. You need to learn how to deal with these people. Easy people are easy. No effort is needed to work with them. So, to all my teachers, past, present, and future: thank you.

To my parents: You instilled in me a work ethic that will forever be a part of who I am and what I am all about. You taught me that giving up was never an option and that hard work pays off. My father passed away at a young age, and I was never really able to thank him personally. Sadly, I don't think I was able to appreciate the greatness of his lessons until well after his passing. Whether intentional or not, his message was received, loud and clear. I also want to thank my mother for letting me use her experiences as subjects for my newspaper articles, this book, and my radio shows. I'm sure she only heard bits and pieces, as she most likely spent more time bragging to her friends that her son was on the radio than actually listening to what I was saying. Thanks a lot for everything. I love you. I know how tough times were, and you always knew when I was going through them myself. You were there when we needed you, and I don't think I can ever truly repay you.

To my mother- and father-in-law: You have been great examples for my wife and me of what love is supposed to look like. No one said being married was supposed to be easy, but you make it look so. I know making a sailing reference would be good here, so here I go…the wake you leave behind makes for a smooth voyage into the future for us. Thank you. Our family has enjoyed a lot of success, from the littlest all the way up, and you are responsible. We love you with all of our hearts.

To my sister: I love you. You are an inspiration and role model to my daughter, as well as women everywhere, and I am proud when you enter a room and I can say you are my sister. I will always be there for you. Although your beauty is fading with age, you will always be gorgeous to me. (You're still my little sister—I can tease, can't I?)

To my sisters- and brother-in-law: Thanks. Best friends are hard to find, even when you have the whole world to pick from; but when you find them in your own family, then that is pretty special.

Thank you to Gisele Benson who, for almost a decade, has made our office one of the happiest places on earth. You are the first thing people see when they walk in, and your smile always lets the clients know that no matter how many financial problems exist in their lives, from now on, everything is going to be okay.

To my assistant, Anna Weiss: You came into my life at exactly the right time and have always proven to me that you had my back. You have brought a sense of peace to my life that I wasn't sure was possible. You are a great assistant, and a better friend.

To Derek Gregoire, Keith Ellis, and Matthew Peck: Thank you. Without you three, none of this was even remotely possible. You allowed me to be my best, and I hope I can become even better. We've always seemed to find a way to not only work together, but be the best of friends. You have proven to me that there is tremendous honor in what we do. Sometimes, our industry can be rightfully criticized for failing to do what is in the client's best interests, opting for its own. Never once in our company's history have I witnessed any of you pondering, for even a second, anything else but the moral and ethical high ground. Our support for one another is the engine that powers us to such great heights. In the words of the girl in Jerry McGuire with the funny smile…"You guys complete me!"

To my children, Madeline, Jacob, and Christopher: You give me life every day. Your energy, spirit, kindness, joy, and love give me my reason to do what I do. I watch your growth with utter amazement and learn from every second we share together. I always thought life was pretty cool, but when you three came around, it became purposeful. There are no cooler, goofier, or more fun wackjobs than you three meatballs! You'll never know how much you mean to me until you have your own to love. I'll never stop kissing those freckles and calling you my babies!

Maddie, my sweet princess, you may have outgrown my lap, but you will never outgrow my heart. I am so proud of who you turned out to be and what you will eventually become. Jake, I heard a great quote about a father's love of his son: "When a father gives to his son, they both laugh. When a son gives to his dad, they both cry." You give me such joy each day I see you accomplish the impossible. Your ability to grow, learn, and discover makes your mom and me so proud to even know you, never mind be your parents. We love you dearly! Christopher, a son is supposed to learn from his dad, but with you, I find myself learning every day from your amazing heart, mind, personality, sense of humor, and spirit. When times are hard and life has got me in a Hulk Hogan figure-four leg lock, then you do something that makes it all better. I wish I knew how you did that! It is obviously a special gift from God, which, coincidentally, is just what you are: a gift from God. I love you, son.

Finally, to my wife, Denise: It is truly hard to even describe the value of what you have meant to me. Jim Carrey once said that behind every man is a woman rolling her eyes. You not only roll your eyes, but still laugh at my silliness from time to time. I know I am not always an easy person to live with, but somehow, you seem to stick it out and take it, day by day. We have been in love since we were children, and we will be this way until the sunset of our glorious life together. The bad times were tough, but thankfully, very few. The good times seem to never end. I love you with all of my heart, soul, skin, toenails, and whatever else I can think of. You know that this isn't a thank-you for helping me write this book, but a thank you for making my life so joyous that I was able to write it. Words were never effective enough tools to express how much you mean to me, but they are all I can use here. So, thank you for being a wonderful mother, incredible friend, and perfect wife.

Finally, to all of you who might pick this book up: read it and then pass it along. The greatest gesture I can get from you is to know that something on these pages resonated enough in your own life that you believed it could be helpful for somebody else. Thanks to all, and happy reading…

Preface

My 11-year-old son was overjoyed to find a metal detector under the Christmas tree this year. It was not a present from Santa Claus, but a thoughtful gift from a younger brother and older sister. As soon as I saw this device, it reminded me of my grandmother, who had recently passed away. Every summer, she would walk the coastline of New Hampshire's Hampton Beach for days with her metal detector, searching for that special lost treasure that she knew would bring her riches. Looking back, however, I am sure that if she had happened upon someone's lost diamond ring, she would have returned it. She would have taken it to the police in hopes that it would find its way back to the finger of its original owner. That's just the kind of person she was. Nevertheless, she diligently scoured the beaches each day, hoping that a heart-stopping discovery would be only a few feet away. She was a child of the Great Depression. What an amazing attitude she had!

Perhaps my son will carry that same hope with him as he plays with his new Christmas toy. Already, he was scanning the grounds of the Nilosek home, looking for the lost treasure buried beneath our South Plymouth, Mass., soil. As I watched him on his quest for buried treasure, it occurred to me that any device is only as useful as the person who operates it. The instructions that came with the metal detector neglected to say that batteries were required, but not included. After fiddling with the device, we rounded up the necessary batteries and he began working with it again, ever hopeful. Another thought crossed my mind: to succeed at any challenging endeavor requires an endless supply of hope. I felt a surge of happiness when I witnessed my wide-eyed son displaying one of his greatest attributes—optimism. He diligently passed the device back and forth over the dirt, still ever hopeful.

What made my grandmother's attitude so remarkable was her belief that life offered hope around every corner. I could see that same spirit reflected in my son. To wake up every morning, knowing that a "treasure" awaits, is a delightful way to live.

In the career path that I have chosen, I deal with many different types of individuals. All of them have money issues of one form or another. We all do. If we have too much money, we have problems. Oh, yes! We have to worry about keeping it and protecting it from loss. If we have too little money, we have problems. If we are in that middle zone, between having too much and having too little, we have problems. Money problems will never disappear. What my clients sometimes fail to see are the full dimensions of their money problems and the strategies they can use to overcome them. A novice will see a vertical cliff as a sheer rock face that cannot be scaled. However, a skilled climber will see the obstacle differently. He or she will immediately begin seeing handholds and footholds. What appears to the one to be a sheer cliff appears to the other to be a scalable climb. It's a matter of training and perception. It is that way with money problems. The handholds and footholds are there and become clearly manifested once pointed out. Finding a solution and solving a problem involving money often requires the same, one-step-at-a-time deliberation and effort, as I hope this book will show.

Life is full of puzzles; each day offers a new set of challenges. Our duty is to face each one squarely on, and find a way to meet and overcome it. For example, someone struggling with the challenge of not having enough money may feel like the person staring up at the rock wall. It may seem as if there is no way to the top. Some of the world's wealthiest people, however, had to overcome obstacles to get where they are. "They probably had some help," a pessimist will whine. Yes, but most successful people recognize when they need help and are not embarrassed or ashamed to admit it. Seeking advice from others is not cheating.

I have found that most people who enjoy enormous wealth have no problem telling others how to get wealthy. You can't walk through a bookstore without seeing hundreds of biographies telling how it can be done. Everyone from Bill Gates to Michael Jordan to Mark Zuckerberg has a story to tell. (Just don't ask Mark about Facebook stock!) People who read and benefit from these success stories will often express gratitude for the lesson and will try to apply it personally, anticipating that they will achieve at least a portion of that success themselves. Interestingly, I cannot recall any of these successful people telling readers that the road to success was a mere walk in the park or "easy as pie." That would be a pretty short book.

I've observed that our nation has developed an ugly personality trait—one that in the past we associated with third-world nations that hate Americans: jealousy. Sometimes, when I find myself in conversation with someone I've just met and I'm asked what I do, I'm immediately dismissed when I answer.

"Oh! Of course, money matters," someone will say, "but not for me, because you see, I have no money." At that point, I sometimes feel the need to offer a motivational speech, à la Tony Robbins. But I usually just let it go. Every single person who reads this has the opportunity to have as much money as he or she desired. It is just a matter of will. Is it easy? No. Not by a long shot. And we like easy, don't we? We want a pill that will make us lose weight. We are intrigued by get-rich-quick formulas. The hard, cold truth is that the road to riches is out there, but you will never see a sign along the shoulder of that road that says No Working Allowed.

In his young heart, my son believes that a treasure exists just below the surface on his next sweep of the metal detector's wand. Little does he know how close it really is. My goal as a father is to make him see that the treasure is not underground, but something he carries inside him every second of every day. I want him to realize that no shiny piece of metal or sack of old coins will ever be as valuable as the hope stored in his heart. I can see his treasure there, but he needs to find it on his own. The very fact that he is looking shows me that it is in there.

Americans need to look inward and regain that same gift for ourselves. We need to believe that no presidential candidate or political figure can solve our problems, nor will any other individual be the reason for our failures. What made America great was that it was built by dreamers who felt that anything was possible. Our country's resume includes such accomplishments as a moon landing, curing countless diseases, and gleaming skyscrapers in bustling cities. We have done great things, and we are capable of even greater things. But the farther we distance ourselves from that spirit of hope and prosperity, the harder it will be to accomplish the great American dream for ourselves.

For as long as I can remember, I have been a person who lives in the future, whether I was sitting in my third grade homeroom waiting impatiently until recess, or thinking about the vacation to Disney World that my family was set to take a few months later. My teachers observed this "daydreaming" and tried their best to wrangle me back into the present. Even in college, I always thought five years into the future. What type of job would I have? What would my wife look like? How many children would fill my home?

Depending on how you look at things, the glass is either half full or half empty. Life has its positives and negatives, and so did my "daydreaming." On the plus side, having a vision of the future has allowed a lot of success to enter my life. Whether you call it the "Law of Attraction" or just having a positive outlook, I've come to be certain that if you think it, it will happen. I have long thought that the human mind has a profound power that works somewhat like a global positioning system (GPS) in your car. Once you set it and plug in the information, the path will be presented to you and you will eventually arrive at your destination. If I program my mind with negative predictions or harmful thoughts, the path before me will most likely manifest these premonitions in my life's events. (I will lay out some examples later in the book on how positive thinking helps the aging process, but for now, take my word for it.)

From a negative standpoint, my type of thinking has made me a prisoner of time. What I mean is that I often neglect the present and fail to enjoy the very moment that I worked so hard to create for myself. As my kids grow up, I often wonder where the time went. How did they get so old and so big? Where was I? I was not working long hours and traveling the world on business, missing the events that make up my kids' lives. I was there. No "Cat's in the Cradle" for me. Almost every single baseball game, dance recital, or school play found me sitting there with a dumb grin plastered on my face and a video camera pressed against my one good eye. But, due to the makeup of my psyche, I programmed myself to constantly look beyond the headlights instead of glancing in the rearview mirror from time to time.

I hope, through the pages of this book, to point out the virtues of slowing down, observing life, and appreciating all the good there is in it. That's what all of the motivational speakers say we should do. I also hope to point out that looking ahead isn't a bad thing. When it comes to retirement and what needs to happen before we enter that special time in our lives, looking ahead could be the difference between a fulfilled life of joy and happiness, or one that's an entree of misery with a side order of regret and despair.

Growing old here in America (assuming that is where you reside) involves a lot of baggage that can, if you let it, make the beautiful process of living a torturous experience. Go with me for a minute… Think with me. The media alone makes the experience of growing older look like a horrible thing to contemplate. Americans spend billions of dollars each year to keep themselves looking, acting, and dressing younger. Whether it's tips on keeping your youthful complexion or surgery to pull, tuck, or remove signs of aging, the attitude seems to be that growing old is something to avoid. With such a negative perception as that in circulation, it's no wonder that people often ignore the steps that must take place so they can age the right way.

Me? I always see the glass as half full. So, most of the tips that will be outlined here in this award-winning American Masterpiece will be worded and presented positively. If we think the right way, we live the right way. Enjoy your experience with this guide, and I hope you refer back to it whenever you find yourself wandering about with a lack of direction.

A Little Bit of History...

A few years back I was asked to write a weekly column for a small local newspaper in Massachusetts. The concept would be based on financial advice for the weekly reader and it wasn't to exceed 1,500 words. Initially I was reluctant to add a new item to my already full agenda. As an owner of a successful financial firm, radio show host, television show host, basketball coach, father, husband, son and friend, I was truly spreading myself too thin. Not "thin" in the nice way where I am comfortably fitting in a seat on a Southwest Airlines plane, but thin in a way in which every waking minute of the day was consumed by some type of responsibility.

My doctor, whom I visited at least once a month for issues pertaining to, let's just say, stress, told me I needed to add a new word to my vocabulary: NO. Every time I was asked to sit on a board of directors, assist a charity, volunteer my time or speak at a local event, I was completely incapable of saying that dreaded word. As you will read in my book, I find life is only properly lived when you say "yes" more often than "No." This was going to be a tough decision. Adding a new responsibility that not required a lot of pre-thought, research, and time, but also had the overwhelming pressure of what great American journalists call the "deadline." That just sounds bad doesn't it? DEAD line. If I wasn't careful I how I lived, I just might be calling into my life the literal meaning of that. My father died at the ripe old age of 62 of a massive heart attack, most likely caused by too much cardiovascular exercise, mixed with an excessive amount of vitamins and minerals. And by "vitamins and minerals," I mean cigarettes and beers. However, as any TV doctor worth their weight would tell you, heart disease runs in families. At least something was running right! Therefore I had to keep a close eye on my lifestyle and get checked out.

What I never really thought was that this opportunity to write would be a welcome release of pent up stress that, if left unchecked, could result in homicidal events that my lawyer would end up blaming on my rough childhood. I grew up in a house that only had four television channels! Not to mention, one of our three TVs had a picture that was black and white!

Managing stress is a full-time job for me. When I hear about the wasteful spending in Washington resulting in more taxes for the Nilosek family, as well as my middle-class brethren, I start to hyperventilate. I am on the radio every day. This means I need to read news stories and hopefully offer some type of end around or financial tip that will solve problems for my audience. Did I mention that I also had to make it entertaining?! You see, it isn't enough to just intelligently highlight the issues, but you need to capture the attention of the audience and make it worth their time to sit and listen. "Infotainment" is the word we use to both have fun but also provide useful tidbits of knowledge that will leave the listener with more productive brain cells than what they started out with. For instance, did you know that New York is the only US state that does not end in the letter "s"? Did you see what I did there? I informed you with the geography question, entertained you with the unique trivial nature of it and then on radio, I reward the eighth caller with a four-pack of tickets to "Disney on Ice" Live at the TD Bank North Garden.

Back in my youth I was a stand-up comedian working clubs and colleges all over the Eastern part of the United States. Obviously I wasn't that good; hence my job now. Being funny was a useful tool to have in that industry. I was known for being the best at having a room full of people simultaneously not smile or laugh. (Actually that is tough to do….try to play the lottery and NOT get one number…..similar skill.) However, it did leave me with the skill of taking life and all of its oddities and communicating the message back with a comical flair. I think I am a lot better at it when people aren't expecting me to be funny first and smart second. Here, if I can relay a point but also make you smile, then I am actually getting something done. For a lot of people, humor is a coping mechanism that lessens the sting of a painful message. I don't care what anyone says, Social Security is hilarious! Re-financing! Ouch, my sides are splitting! Pre-paid funerals – stop you're killing me! (Did I actually just say that?) These are the things that people NEED to learn about but who in their right mind will take the time to read about Required Minimum Distributions with their Sunday morning cup of coffee? So what can I do to make this topic interesting? Well, sit back, grab a bottle of wine, relax and enjoy…

CHAPTER ONE

To Succeed at Old Age, You Have to Start Young

"If you don't know where you are going, any road will get you there."

— Lewis Carroll

I am a sufferer of a disease called Attention Deficit Disorder. Disease might be a bit harsh. Condition? Better. The bottom line is that I have a tough time staying on task or remaining focused. Hey, did you see Dancing with the Stars last night? Sorry. See what I mean?

From time to time, I may wander off in a few different directions. First, a comment on ADD: I am not the type of scatterbrain who uses this label as a crutch to do unfocused crazy things and then blame it on something. I think everyone in the country is saying they have ADD because they have trouble staying focused. That is based more on our culture than an actual imbalance of chemicals in the brain. We are the nation of 10 minutes or less. I can cook a microwave dinner in 3 seconds! The Cosby family could solve a huge domestic crisis in 28 minutes. Television commercials are made to sell us cars, soup, dog food and candy in 30 seconds. I like to call us the MTV generation. (Sadly even that makes me sound old!) The image has to shift or change every two seconds or we're bored out of our minds. This plays a major role in how we receive our information in the new age of media. The television news plays clips of a presidential candidate's speech that consist of quick sound bites that may only contain a total of 25 words! From that, we feel prepared and armed to walk into the voting booth and pull the lever for the next ruler of the free world. If you subscribe to the notion of humans constantly evolving to fit into the circumstances and environment around them, then we are on the fast track to being totally unable to think for ourselves.

Famed comedian George Carlin did a whole bit about how kids should be forced to stare out of the window into space for one hour every day. His point was that we have denied our kids the ability to daydream and wonder. When I was a kid, my sister and I sat in the back seat of the family car and stared at trees and clouds as we traveled down the highway. We didn't have DVD players playing movies the entire time. Our entertainment was trying not to throw up from being carsick! Now I look back as I drive and not only are my kids all watching movies or playing video games, but they all have their own devices. Sitting in the back seat of a car talking on a cell phone should be reserved for Heads of State and Kings, not 11 year olds in Iron Man T-shirts!

My point it that ADD is over diagnosed and sometimes placed in a context in which it doesn't belong. That being said, I have it and I have the medical records available to prove it. I had to take tests to get to that point and it wasn't until my late 30s that I had a definitive answer from a medical professional confirming what I suspected.

As a reader you might be wondering why this is even relevant to the book. Don't worry, I won't be getting into my other medical conditions, but if you happen to know of any over-the-counter powerful rash cream, I might like to get my hands on a tube…

I say this about the ADD because the book is going to appear to be all over the place. Some of it is because of the ADD. Most of it is because I am taking different subjects that I have tackled over the last 52 weeks in my newspaper column and building a complete novel. I like that you as a reader can follow my journey through the year and see what was pressing on certain random weeks. This book will contain numerous themes. The main one will be financially based. Money is a very important part of our everyday existence. We teach our kids that life isn't about money and we should not worship it, yet hammer into them the notion that if you fail in school you won't get a good job and might wind up living on the streets. We demonize people who have too much of it but then all fight to get lottery tickets promising record payouts. We have a love-hate relationship with money. We want Wall Street to be productive but also want the bums thrown into jail! We want jobs but want the CEOs hung from trees in the public square. So which is it? Do we love money or hate it?

I think this book will stress that it isn't the money itself that we love, but it is what we do with it that matters. A hundred dollar bill can buy enough booze to kill a man but also provide a lavish meal to an underprivileged family. Money is a symbol and hard proof of the effort and sacrifice you put into your working years. I never thought I would say this, but the notion of having a strong work ethic is sadly becoming a thing of the past. I remember when a day's pay was a result of putting 8-10 hours of backbreaking work out there and then feeling an overwhelming sense of accomplishment. Now people demand handouts, government entitlements and free money without even the slightest bit of shame.

What's in it for me? How do I get money from the government? This country is on the path to falling into oblivion like the great Roman Empire did centuries ago. Once the number of citizens in this country who are suckling off the government teat exceeds that of the working class then we have, as so many economist have put it, reached the tipping point. The tipping point means the voting majority has an interest in making sure their handouts, tax-free rides and entitlements continue. Why would you vote for government accountability and reduced spending when you need that for your spending money?

The nation will not be able to survive if it continues down the path it is on. I'm sure I am not breaking any news with that declaration. If we expect the United States to be in business in 30 years, we need to make changes. This book will not be focused on what we need to do as voters but as individuals. How do we use the news and fears of the day to better arm our own households to withstand the storm? Our elected officials all seem to think running the budget of the country is less important than the budget of their own homes. If they conducted their personal finances like the United States government, they would have never been elected in the first place. You and I are forced to live in a world where if the electric bill is not paid, the lights go out. If you don't get good grades in school, then you don't move onto the next level. If you eat too much, then you get fat. But you know as well as I that our culture feels that if you can't pay your electric bill then get in line for handouts; if you fail in school then rather than be held back, students are sent along regardless of what they know. And my favorite, if you get fat, just sue the fast food joint that kept selling you the burgers and shakes.

Getting a hold of your personal situation is vital to living a healthy, happy retirement. Each chapter will be an important topic, relevant to most of you. I hope to present a different perspective and spin that might make you think about things in a whole new way.

I find that with most of my clients, if you are able to sum up the planning process in one easy to understand example, then the seemingly overwhelming task of taking on everything can be made easy to swallow. Go with me on a little journey of make-believe. Imagine that you are standing in a barn with chickens, goats, and cows. Over in the corner there is a little three-legged milking stool on which the farmer will sit to milk ole' Bessie. Take that stool and place it in the center of the barn and stand on it. How does it feel? Is it secure? Or do you feel it wobble a bit? Are any of the legs loose, or about to fall off? Retirement can be likened to a three legged stool, and your answers about the way that stool feels can tell us a great deal about your retirement picture. Each leg of the stool represents a key element of your retirement, and if one leg is off just a tad, it can cause a tragic chain reaction that can rip apart all of your hard work.

The three legs are financial, legal and health. If one of these areas are compromised, or encounters some unexpected troubles, then doom and gloom might not be too far behind. As an example, if you should suffer a health condition, it could be the most costly financial event of your life. Retirees are finding that if they are unprepared for it, a nursing home stay can be financially devastating. On average, in the New England area, a private room in a nursing facility can run you over $300 per day. That's $9000 per month, or $108,000 per year. Yikes! According to the industry experts, the average length of time a person may spend in a nursing facility, assisted living, home care or some type of rehabilitation is 3.5 years. So if you have been taking notes and doing the math, that comes out to over $350,000! How long could an average household go before they are completely broke? Don't forget that these figures are averages. Some people might be looking at 10 to 15 years in a nursing facility if they suffer from Alzheimers or demintia. Others might be looking at just a few months. It is impossible to predict.

From the leg that represents the financial side, it is easy to see where trouble might loom. It never ceases to amaze me that if you were to poll 2000 people, 100% of them would admit that the stock market is a good place to lose money. Over the long run (the very long run), you might be okay investing straight up in the stock market. But for people in their 50s, 60s, or 70s who plan to retire in the near future, the stock market can become a horrible whirlpool of doom. If you had wanted to retire in 2008, there would have been a better than average chance that if you started pulling income out of your nest egg, you were doing so at a 50% disadvantage. Even though everybody knew it was a good possibility that the market could go down, those same people still thought "never me!" Having one's head in the sand is not conducive to effectively running the ball in the forth quarter of life!

The financial leg also ties into health when individuals deprive themselves of health options in life because of a lack of monthly income. Often you will find that the most expensive foods in a grocery store are the healthy options. Organic grocery stores tend to stock high end products that carry a high end cost. Health club memberships cost money. Making regular trips to the doctor, dentist, and other specialists costs money. Prescription programs through Medicare cost money. Without money, people eat poorly, suffer more health issues, and may be overly stressed. Is that a generality? Sure. But the eyeball test tells it like it is.

All of the clients that walk through my door are given, at no charge, a free lesson in believing the "Quality of Life" principle, which states that you have one go around on this blue marble and you can't take it with you; therefore it is counter-productive to leave money behind and deprive yourself of the fruits of life. Yes, we want to take care of our families after we depart, but wouldn't it be nice to do so while we are here? I would much rather see my grandchildren's smiling faces as we toured the parks of Disney World, than to have them do so after my death with the proceeds from a paper check from a life insurance policy.

CHAPTER TWO
Make "Planning" Number One on your To-Do List

"Finish each day and be done with it. You have done what you could. Some blunders and absurdities no doubt crept in; forget them as soon as you can. Tomorrow is a new day. You shall begin it serenely and with too high a spirit to be encumbered with your old nonsense."

— Ralph Waldo Emerson

I love it when people approach me and ask me questions about something they heard on my radio or TV show. First of all, it gives me an inner peace to know that people are actually listening and watching, and that all of my hard work is paying off. But to a greater degree I feel like the little things I discuss, either in my print columns or on my radio and television programs, actually do make a difference in people's lives.

When I first got into the financial business, it was out of pure desperation. The only reason I decided to go through a training program at an insurance company was so that I could learn something about the world of finance. I felt totally helpless and inept when I would call my health insurance provider to ask a question, and realize that I did not understand one thing about my own coverage. I also felt like a failure when I looked at my savings account and realized that I didn't have anything there. "How do I make a change and get things going on the right track?" I wondered.

The usual answer you get when you ask such a question goes something like this: "Spend as little as possible and save as much as you can." Wow! Profound financial advice from the money guru, right? But the truth of the matter is, that little piece of advice could be the push you need to begin laying a foundation for a healthy, productive financial future. Financial freedom isn't just from "how much" cash you have coming in the door. It's the action you take today to make your future days worth something.

I am about to give you a guide or a series of steps to follow to get you on the right path. You will then be entertained, and educated with different areas of the financial world.

Step 1- JUMP IN!

This is the hardest step to take because it usually involves blindly going where you have never stepped before. It is scary and is usually avoided with excuses…more important things like having to pick up the dry-cleaning. This step is where most people totally fall down. Just like losing weight and going to the gym, the first visit is the hardest. Once you get into the habit of getting your fat butt to the gym, it is totally easy from there. So many of the clients that walk into our offices have said that they had heard us on the radio for YEARS before they took the initiative to come in. As for my firm, we make the first step very easy. You don't have to prepare, or know a thing, when you walk through the door. It is a conversation that involves zero work on your part. Most people really appreciate this. The tension is removed, and they are more open to talking and expressing how they feel and what they are trying to accomplish.

Step 2- Item Check list.

Now that the hard part is out of the way, we think, for lack of a better term, that it is all downhill from here! In the financial world saying "downhill" might be frowned upon, but I look at it like being able to take your foot off the gas pedal, relax and coast your way into a comfortable retirement. The second step involves making a list, or taking inventory of what it is that makes up your photo album of life. Who are the faces in those pictures? What are the activities you like to take part in? Where do you live? Where do you travel? What did you do for a living?

These factors are what builds a proper retirement strategy. It isn't the rate of return or the highest value of a stock that makes for success. It is whether you are living - and I mean truly "living"- your life to the fullest.

The results or scorecard, of who you are, what you did, and whom you love are, to a small degree, reflected in your legal documents, estate plan, financial accounts and real estate. Your retirement plan needs fuel to power its way through the deep mud ahead. The items used to power you through are the assets you have built up in your savings and retirement accounts up until now.

For clients of our firm, the second step involves, taking an inventory of everything in your life that makes you who you are. It sounds like a big chore doesn't it? Actually it isn't. We accomplish this step in under an hour. Once your financial professional has the full picture, they can officially begin. If they don't ask all of those questions, then not only do they not know who you are, and what you are all about, but they also have no idea of where you need to be headed in the next 30 years. This step is where so many financial professionals drop the ball, and cease being useful. I get a strange look from some when I ask what their hobbies are. "Why do you need to know....or care what I like to do in my free time?" First of all, I care because as a client (this is going to sound cheesey) I actually do care about you as an individual. If during that first meeting we somehow can't muster up the ability to care about you personally, then you are most likely a disaster, and not equipped to be in public. I say that because it is rare for us not to like someone. Another reason I care about you and your hobbies/interests is that they might have a significant impact on the financial plan you want to build. If you are 55 years old, insisting on retiring at age 65, then how much you have in your plan will vary a great deal if your hobby is sailing, for example, instead of baking. If you are a collector of antique muscle cars, and you travel the country looking for original parts in your restoration project, then we might want to view this as a very expensive lifestyle. I also might want to educate you on certain aspects of tax planning that can helps people with expensive hobbies.

Another part of caring is making your experience as a client of our firm a special one. We want to make the process of working with us not only financially rewarding, but memorable and pleasant. That way you will not only feel comfortable calling us when you need to, but you will refer your family and friends.

STEP 3- Evaluate where you are on the map

Plan According To Your Age

What action should you be taking? It really depends on the time of life in which you find yourself right now. Someone in their 20s and 30s is deals with things from a much different perspective than someone in their 60s and 70s. For someone approaching retirement in the next five to ten years, his or her foundation should be income and safety. How much money do I need each month to live on? How do I make sure that over time, those dollar values will keep up with inflation? What planning steps do I need to make now so that I never run out?

Retirees shudder at the thought of living to age 90 and beyond, and losing their independence because they ran out of money. To give you an idea of just how ingrained this fear is, I have had conversations with retirees who have been told by their financial advisor that it is virtually impossible to run out of money at the rate they are spending now. Even so, the retiree still fears running out of money so much that they life a life of what I would deem self-imposed poverty. No one wishes to become vulnerable because they didn't plan properly. Believe it or not, some people plan to a certain date, as if they can predict when they will die. Not only is that creepy and unhealthy; it is not necessary. In today's financial marketplace, it is quite easy to plan for a lifetime of income with guarantees protecting you as long as you life – even if you live to age 150.

Why doesn't everybody take this safe, easy road to success? Well, for one thing, we live a world where Wall Street and the media spends billions of dollars to make us think a certain way. We have been brainwashed by the government, big business, and Wall Street to subscribe to a certain way of thinking – one that focuses more on their pockets than it does on ours.

For the young planner, the focus can be more long-term and geared more towards risk. But the foundation should still be laid with concrete ideas and proven methods to ensure protection during times of trouble. Savings accounts with six months of cash are an excellent idea, but not always practical. Most young adults with whom I am acquainted live from month-to-month, and from hand-to-mouth. Things are more expensive today, true. But there are also expenses that didn't exist 15 years ago. Bills for such things as cable TV, Internet service, smart phones, bottled water, and other "must haves" relentlessly tap our resources.

So what can you "kids" do? For one thing, pay attention to your credit picture. If possible, make sure your credit score is the highest it can be. Study how it works. Learn the tricks. The money you can save here is like putting money into an IRA. Some people overpay on their bills by as much as $1,500 per month. If my math is correct, that is $18,000 per year. In just three years, that is enough money to generate $155,400 of growth, and an income of $2,590 per month for 60 months starting in 2024. If you are keeping track, that is a 7.5% rate of return. (The figures used to calculate that income stream were based on an actual case made available by SHP Financial that offered a guaranteed effective interest rate over that period of time through the use of a pre-owned annuity, or structured settlement.) Those are real numbers folks.

STEP 4- Who are the partners in your plan?

Sounds like an easy answer right? It's me and the spouse. Right? Normally I'd say, correct. Your 401(k) has both your names on there in some capacity. But beneath the small print, tucked deep within the tax codes of our annually released IRS laws, is another name that you had no idea about. Your Uncle. Uncle Sam. Never forget that when you open a qualified account such as a

401(k), 403(b) or IRA, you assume partnership with the US government. It is a great deal for Uncle Sam, but so much for you. Think about it. You are working hard, putting money away, and agreeing to take some tax benefits now, but agreeing that you will cut Uncle Sam in on the deal when you turn 59 ½. The big problem I see with what Uncle Sam wants, is that there is no way to know what your share is, or what goes to him, because it is all based on an income tax rate that will adjust many times along the way. Uncle Sam has the best deal! Not only does he have his hand in your cookie jar, but in effect, he can change the rules along the way to get more in the long run. Here is an example. If you had $400,000 now in a pre-tax, qualified account and you decided to retire today, about 50% of it would most likely go to taxes. Half of your money would never make it into your hands. Between state and federal tax obligations, you are looking at having roughly $200,000 left for you and and your spouse. Uncle Sam gets 50%, you get 25%, and your spouse gets 25%. Hmm, but you did 100% of the work!

If you decided to retire 20 years from now, you would need to take a guess on what the income tax rate is going to be. Considering the fact that historians put the current income tax rate at an all time low, it is safe to assume that rates will be higher in the future, when you retire, than they are now. During World War II, if more than $200,000 per year you could have been paying over 90% in income tax! Don't believe me? Google it. With the direction in our country is heading, and how dim the long term forecast is, I don't think a 90% tax rate is likely in the future, but a tax hike is certainly in the cards.

Pay Tax on the Seed, Not the Harvest

Younger people should also be subscribing to the concept of paying taxes now rather than deferring them to a later time. How in the world did the financial powers that be ever convince us that it is better to be taxed later instead of now? Who thinks the tax rate will be higher in the next five to 10 years? Who thinks the government will erase a 1.5 trillion-dollar deficit in the next 20 years? Who believes that congress will solve the problems that exist with Social Security, Medicare, and, while they are at it, end all conflicts beyond our borders?

Taxes are going up, so planning for it is smart and will create money in the future that you don't need to have in hand now. If you were a farmer, would you rather pay taxes on the seed you plant into the ground, or the harvest it yields down the road? The answer is obvious, but how many young people still pack all of their monthly savings into an IRA? Keep in mind that when you want to retire, a $500,000 IRA is only worth as much as the current tax rate. As of the writing of this book, that $500,000 is only worth half that amount. That is an absurd way to invest to me. How do you expect to plan when you don't know what the rules will be in 20 years? Planning for a tax-free retirement is not only wise but also getting to be a common school of thought that will eventually be the rule of thumb as time goes by.

I always direct my clients to read Tax Free Retirement, written by bestselling author Patrick Kelly. The book outlines the theory for and introduces the concept of tax-free retirement to a population that has to forget EVERYTHING they ever learned about saving, and think in a new way. (I have the book and it would be my pleasure to loan it out to anyone who is sincerely interested) Now is the time we need to think of these things.

Regardless of your age, you need to lay the foundation to create the most productive, efficient, realistic retirement plan you can. I know you can do it, and I believe in you.

In 1861, our country had a problem. The Union needed money to fund the war effort against the Confederacy. So the simple solution was to create a new tax called the Revenue Act of 1861. Little did they know that this simple act of congress would become one of the most fought over political issues in 2012. Income tax in the United States is such a powder keg, that it even sparked the emergence of a whole new political movement known as the "Tea Party".

However, as we all stress over the burden the IRS places on us, it is important to know that we sit at one of the lowest tax rates on average in the history of our great nation. How could that be? Why are we so hung up on taxes then?

The CBO or Congressional Budget Office reported in 2009 that the average household paid 17.4 % of its income to the federal government.

That figure sits 20% lower than what the average was during the Regan years. The obvious flaw with the numbers is that the 17.4% is an average. According to the report, the "wealthy" pay a disproportionately larger share of all taxes while "non-wealthy" people pay nothing at all. Culturally, we have decided that those who pay the most that should absorb the wrath heaped upon those who are to blame. Although that isn't logical, it is easy to look back in history and see how this negative trait in human nature can be powerful enough to bring down a society. Actually you don't even have to look back in time, just overseas to the economic crisis occurring in Europe.

A little factoid that you may find useful at the next cocktail party you attend is that the highest income tax rate our country every experienced was 94% back during World War II for people who earned more than $200,000 per year. Ouch!

The obvious solution to the whole tax mess is to broaden the base of people who pay taxes to the point where at least everyone pays something. Rich or poor, moving the country forward should be the mission of every American.

Let's table this argument for the time being. I think that most of us would agree that combating government waste and mismanagement of our dollars is the biggest problem. Before we start the whole "raise taxes on the workers" movement again, or, as it was called a year ago, Occupy Wall Street, we should ask how we, according to a recent US audit, wasted $200 million on "useless" Iraqi police training. Or how a $2 billion road project swelled into $22 billion (if not paid off by 2038) in Massachusetts at the same time citizens voted to increase the income tax rate. Tough decisions mean tough leaders and tough leaders need citizens to be smart about who they elect.

From a personal finance standpoint, I worry about the number of people who rely totally on their tax qualified retirement accounts for their future income needs that are being thrust into the crosshairs of this maddening debate. US News and World Report said that in the year 2012, Americans were experiencing what it called a tax bargain. Wouldn't it appear likely that a tax increase for "wealthy" retirees would be the next move our government makes, as opposed to curtailing its own wasteful spending?

This uncertain threat makes it pretty hard for a financial professional like myself to plan for your income.

So what do you do?

I am seeing more and more people today taking the wise step of paying taxes now, while the rate is at historic lows, so they can enjoy a more tax-friendly position down the line. Like I said before, you must ask yourself if it seems likely that taxes will go up in the future. Obviously, I have no way of predicting what the future holds. I also can't begin to predict what our politicians will do, let alone the voters. I hate to harp on the state income tax vote that I personally witnessed recently, but when presented with the option to increase taxes or leave them alone, people choose the former. Fewer people thought that that curbing spending was needed, even when we just witnessed the greatest fraud of public spending over the last 20 years in the form of Boston's "Big Dig".

For the younger readers of this book, I suggest you try to plan to be as tax free as possible. Step one is to focus in on the idea of taxing the "seed" rather than the "harvest." Isn't it a safer bet to assume that you will have more tax write offs and deductions in your younger years than you will later on in life. Also, consider that the laws may change. Deductions and exemptions that exist now may not be available when you retire. Many would be surprised to know that removing the mortgage interest deduction, which tends to be the biggest deduction on the tax returns of most young people, is being batted around by lawmakers. The point is we have no idea what is going to happen, but we do know what is happening now. The tax land mine is just as important to plan for as failing health, income and market fluctuations. Personally, I am tired of the worry and fear that some government corruption, political inside deal, or a deadly dose of Chicago-style politics will derail what I have worked so hard to build up.

There is only so much you can do when you get behind the curtain to cast your vote. Let's just hope that the gold in your life is for the golden years and not the golden arches.

CHAPTER THREE
Why You Must Plan for a Specific Income

"When a man retires, his wife gets twice the husband but only half the income."

-Chi Chi Rodriguez

"Income" just might be the most significant word uttered in any financial planning meeting. Why? Well, the whole reason why we save and work so hard during our younger years is so we can sit back, relax and let our nest egg provide for us in our later life.

When planning to receive income, it is vital to consider a few crucial factors, the first of which is expenses. Obviously, your income needs to be sufficient to pay your ongoing bills, such as utilities, food, insurance, rent and taxes. Once we exhaust income from Social Security and other pension sources, we need an income plan to step in and cover the rest.

A Strong Financial Foundation Will Last

When we saw the aftermath of Hurricane Katrina from satellite photos of the Gulf Coast, the visual image we could not forget was that of thousands of concrete foundations where homes once sat. Even after the all the violence that Mother Nature could unleash, those concrete foundations remained.

A financial storm can take the form of a market crash, a health crisis or inflation. We saw one of the biggest financial storms of all time in 2008. The sudden decline in the stock market left in ruins the financial houses of millions of Americans – that is, unless, they had been wise enough to have a solid financial foundation.

Income should be that guaranteed foundation that will withstand any massive financial catastrophe that may hit us blindly on a random Tuesday afternoon. Keep in mind: our bills do not stop; our desire to eat does not leave us, and our health will most likely still need attention. Once you lay the proper foundation, then you can safely embark on a financial avenue of risk if you wish. But I still advise caution. Fortunately, for my partners and me, risk is something we avoid altogether. Risk is a luxury that some can't afford. The question you must ask yourself is, "How much money can I afford to lose before I am left with just the basic foundation of income?"

Aim Specifically

I find that in today's world, income planning involves a lot more than just "shooting" for an interest rate that we hope will ensure that we never run out of money. It involves so much more. The notion of running out of money before we die is one of the most common fears people face as they age. Study after study confirms that those of the general public worry more about outliving their income than they do about premature death. So if you could trigger a plan in which your accounts never stop producing income - even if you live to be 130 years of age - would you do it? Well, yes and no. There are pros and cons to every financial move. But selecting a guaranteed lifetime income payout might be just the thing needed to enable you to sleep well at night. The other side of the coin is that some of those plans offer little in the way of flexibility and choice. Since life is not that simple, I will often set up income plans in more manageable chunks, like five to seven years. The objective is to try and figure out our income needs today, and then give ourselves a decent raise every 12 months, while ensuring that the ending value of our account is equal to or greater than what we started with.

Example: Client invests $500,000 and lives off of $20,000 per year (4%). We need to ensure that the money is earning more than 4% to prevent a dip into the principle. So if Mr. and Mrs. Client are in a structured settlement investment that earns 5%, then we have just hit the income grand slam – adequate income, inflation protection and an increased bottom line to work with while we set up the next phase of planning. (Note that SHP Financial is the only firm in the New England area with access to these cases as they are only available on a limited basis. Settlement transfers are secondary market investments that are court ordered, guaranteed investments that often provide returns far greater than the current marketplace. SST's are also case-by-case transactions similar to the purchase of a house or boat. Therefore, SHP may only have a limit of 50-60 cases available per week. They are not at risk investments, like a mutual fund or a stock purchase. STT's are guaranteed payments from the result of a lawsuit, or other court decided award.)

There are also many options other than structured settlements that can guarantee the accomplishment of similar goals. How about an income annuity that offers a head start bonus along with minimums that lock in certain income guarantees? These options generally vary from month to month as the industry adapts to current economic conditions, but with the help of a competent income specialist you might well be on your way to "income bliss!"

Choosing the Right Income Model

Age, health and marital status are also vital factors in building the right income model. Ask yourself, "What income plan do I have right now?" Be sure that your financial specialist deals with income separately. Growing your money and spending your money have to work side by side, but having an accumulation strategy from which you intend to pull income might just be mixing oil and water.

It is imperative to recognize the phase you are in and maximize it. If you are still trying to build up your nest egg, and your investment horizon exceeds 15 years, then taking risk should be a key part of your decision making. However, if you are within 15 years of retirement, then it makes sense to re-evaluate your game plan and adjust accordingly. Ask anyone who was planning to retire in the winter of 2008, and see if they were happy with the outcome. Unless they had a plan, I would say they were not.

Game Plan

The following is an article I wrote recently on the importance of having a good game plan. Even though the article ran in the summer of 2012, six months after my beloved New England Patriots lost the Super Bowl, I still felt it might not be the worst thing to include the "Patriot Way" in the theme. I know there are a lot of Patriot haters around the country, so if you are one of them, as you read it, just substitute references to the Patriots with whatever embarrassing team (just kidding) it is that you support. Here's the article:

What's Your Game Plan?

Let's face it. Since the turn of the new century there has really been one word that best describes the attitudes of the American people - pessimistic. Almost every person that comes into my office these days seems to be searching for some type of respite from the bad news that is hitting us like an unrelenting hail storm. I am not innocent in the blame game when it comes to reporting bad news. On all of my radio shows, TV shows, in my newspaper column and speeches that I am asked to give, I can't help but start them all with three or four of the latest miserable stories breaking on the wire.

Take this month for instance. The constitutionality of Obamacare was recently challenged and upheld by the highest court in the land resulting in a continued migraine for business owners and employers. The June employment numbers were down again, showing that the recovery isn't going as planned, and the looming fiscal cliff still seems to be the most ignored massive news story of all time! This is just July!

The housing meltdown, Europe, political gridlock, government waste aside, there is still a lot of good news for us to appreciate. In the medical community, when a disease becomes too predominant in society, researchers work on cures and treatments. If the disease didn't bother the human race enough; it would have been left alone. The financial marketplace is no different. The resulting "treatments" and "cures" for all that is plaguing us as citizens are now becoming a big part of the way we plan. My business, SHP Financial, was built on satisfying a segment of the population who wishes to insulate itself from market loss and unnecessary risk. We began in 2003, after the market meltdown of 2001 and 2002, and, believe it or not, I don't think the public was ready for us at the time. For whatever reason, the American public assumed that the market hit experienced back in 2002 was just a strange occurrence resulting from the 2011 terrorist attacks. The thought never crossed their minds that market volatility and world uncertainty would remain a constant for years to come. Sadly, that lesson we could have learned back then would have been an extremely valuable one to benefit from when the 2008 market crash devastated so many. The question remains still. Are you prepared for the next market event that experts predict will be worse than the last two combined?

In some respects, pessimism can be a good thing. However, when the reaction to pessimism is a lack of action, or paralysis, then it becomes your worst enemy. I have said for a long time that one of the best lessons we can take from the past decade of chaos is to put more emphasis on good game planning. If the New England Patriots were playing the Silver Lake Lakers in a football game, I'm sure Bill Belichik would spend little to no brain power on setting up a game plan, knowing full well that they could win comfortably on their talent alone. Yet if they were playing the New York Giants, he would spend every second setting up a well thought out game plan that would cover every possible contingency. The challenges that we face in our economy today are worth the time and effort spend developing a game plan. Too much is on the line for us not to plan.

Here at SHP Financial, we focus on those game plans that will have successful results, despite the negative data we stare at daily. Most modern financial planners should be presenting you whole new concepts and strategies that can be modified to fit the challenges we face. , If they are not doing that for you, then you really need to ask why not. Don't forget, you are the CEO and President of your own financial plan. Your advisor is working for you. So if they are not WORKING to show you different routes or angles then you might want to consider finding a new quarterback!

Looking at your advisor like a GPS is a good analogy. You paid good money to have this device sit atop your dashboard and tell you where to go. It is of great value to you if everything is seamless. When you get to your destination with no troubles, you feel great. Your advisor serves the same function. You want them to get you to where you need to be. If you don't know where you need to be, then asking where you want to be is vital.

Don't let the troublesome news of the day ruin your future because of fear of planning. Use the prompting of the media to motivate you to take action and set up a plan. Worst-case scenario is you sat with a professional and got nothing out of it. What did you lose an hour, two? Best-case scenario, you secured your future retirement needs.

I will continue to talk about the fiscal cliff, deficit, employment, Europe, Social Security, government waste, taxes, fraud, Wall Street and the like, but this time when you hear something that makes you ill, you will know that your pessimism turned into a plan and your plan turned into success. Once you insulate yourself and your family from the troubles of 2012 then nothing can stop you from a future of great things.

CHAPTER FOUR

The Truth about Tax-Deferred Savings Plans

"But better to be hurt by the truth than comforted with a lie."
— Khaled Hosseini

I know I just covered this a few chapters before, but it is such a vitally important topic that you may see touch on it a few more times through this book.

Stop me if you have heard this, "Everyone should be putting as much money away as possible into your IRA or 401(k)!" I'll start off by making the assumption that most of my readers know what an IRA or 401(k) is. But if not, here it is. An IRA, or Individual Retirement Account, is a type of retirement saving plan that offers the owner some specific tax benefits. There are two types of IRA's, Traditional and Roth. Both allow you to contribute up to a certain amount per year and both offer you the advantage (or disadvantage, depending on your point of view) of tax deferral. You may wish to check with your financial professional to determine just how much you are allowed to contribute to these accounts annually. That amount may vary based on some individual factors. A traditional IRA allows the investor to put money aside and get some present-day tax benefits. A Roth IRA is funded with money that has already been taxed. Then the proceeds and growth may be received on a tax-free basis in the future. The problem with Roth accounts is that if you earn "too" much money, or your MAGI (Modified Adjusted Gross Income) is above the threshold, then it might not even be an option. For both accounts, you cannot begin withdrawing money penalty-free from your account until you are 59 ½. Even if you have not collected anything from your account, you will be required to take withdrawals when you reach age 70 ½. These are called Required Minimum Distributions, or RMD's.

Getting the Most Out of Your 401(k)

A 401(k) is named after a specific line of the tax code that allows an employer to make contributions on behalf of employees and receive certain tax advantages. The 401(k) is most beneficial to the employee when the company not only makes the deduction from the paycheck each week and deposits it into the account, but also matches the contribution up to a certain level. Since the economic collapse of 2008, many companies, in efforts to reduce costs and avoid layoffs, have either ceased making matching contributions or curtailed them significantly. It is a good idea to know whether or not your company is still matching because it might be the deciding factor in whether you continue with that investment or move on to greener pastures.

The problem with these qualified accounts is that the selling point or advantage of today might be the poison of tomorrow. IRAs, 401(k)s, 403(b)s, or any of the other so-called tax-favored accounts, are delaying an issue that most of us have no control over – taxes. Millions of Americans are investing in accounts and have no idea what those accounts will look like on the back end. Yes, they may know that they have $500,000 set aside, and that, in a few years, it should be roughly that same amount still, but because they are delaying the consequences of paying the tax, they may be setting themselves up for a major unpleasant surprise on the back end.

What About Taxes?

At this writing, tax rates are at an all time low, so it's safe to say that the climate of the country, as I am writing this, seems to indicate a future fraught with tax increases. Social Security is in turmoil, Medicare is overwhelmed, federal debt is in the trillions, state budgets are out of control and the country is waging costly foreign wars. All of these situations are typical of those which breed higher taxes.

I believe we have reached a point in history where we had better start thinking outside of the box if we expect to someday enjoy success. We need to take what the world is telling us and make changes accordingly. We must adapt to our surroundings. Is it such a stretch to believe that paying taxes now might be better than paying taxes in the future? I don't have any magic spell that helps you avoid that April 15th ulcer. Death and taxes, right?

The area of New England where I live is known for its' beautiful farms and rich traditions. Next time you tour Plimoth Plantation or Old Sturbridge Village, ask the farmers if they would rather pay the tax on the seed they plant into the ground or the harvest that they reap in the fall. They will take the seed option every time. It's no different for us today. Would you not rather pay a tax, at an assumed lower rate now, on the money you save at work, than pay taxes on the total growth, at your retirement age when the tax rate might be sky high? If you think that taxes are on the way down, then please consult a doctor and turn your keys over to the Registry of Motor Vehicles. You shouldn't be on the roads! But if you can read the handwriting on the wall ,and believe that taxes may go up, then it might not be a bad idea to broaden your portfolio and include some tax free savings plans. In subsequent chapters, I will get into different strategies that allow people to take advantage of proven tax favorable accounts that will keep you and the IRS man at arms' length.

401(k)s, IRAs and other investments are all excellent tools to help us accomplish great things. But by themselves, they must be looked at in the context of the prevailing economic conditions of the time in which they exist. Every financial vehicle has its place and value. It is never a smart idea to dismiss any idea or plan just because your neighbor is doing something different. Consult a financial professional and check out your opinions. Your retirement goals and dreams are too important for you to simply follow the herd.

CHAPTER FIVE

Building a Case for Tax-Free Income

"Think Different"

-Apple

Before you rip this page out of the book and put it in the bottom of the birdcage, promise me that you will at least give what follows a chance to be read. I'm going to talk about a few things you have probably never considered when it comes to…hold on…brace yourself…life insurance.

Are you there? Did I lose you?

Good. I'm glad you hung out for a bit and gave me the benefit of the doubt here. I truly think this is going to give you a whole new appreciation for life insurance and its value. We all know that life insurance was designed to give us a safety net in case the worst happens. If we die, our loved ones will be taken care of and their needs will be met in our absence. Purchasing that kind of insurance is both a responsible thing to do and a smart financial move. Of course, one of the main reasons people fail to do this is because, when you think about it, you are shelling out cash, probably in a tough economy, on something you hope you will never need. What I am about to do, is put the "life" back into life insurance.

For too long, we have looked at Life Insurance as death insurance. As a marketing guy, I find that one of the biggest mistakes the insurance industry ever made was to create that impression among the general population. I recently sat down with wealth strategist and life insurance expert Keith Ellis from SHP Financial of Plymouth, Massachusetts, who pointed out that there are multiple purposes for life insurance other than just the one with which everyone is so familiar.

Point number one – Most Americans have no idea that income from a life insurance policy is tax-free in the eyes of the IRS. For the last few decades, whole life insurance has evolved into a truly useful investment, allowing people to protect principle while earning competitive interest, and at the same time providing a well-needed, tax-free, probate-free death benefit.

You may be aware of the fact that America, as of this writing, anyway, is in some financial hot water. The only real solution Washington seems to have is to generate revenue from – you guessed it – taxes.

"It's safe to assume that taxes will be on the rise," said Ellis, explaining that he often talks to his young and concerned clients about implementing a retirement plan that includes a tax-free income stream.

I often wonder how people can calculate what their income will be when they have tax deferred accounts, like 401(k)s, IRAs or 403(b)s. Let's say you have $400,000 in a retirement account and you plan to use that money to live on once you retire. Unless you know what the tax rate is going to be 20 years from now, how can you be expected to plan? Ellis encourages young people to tax the "seed" rather than the "harvest". This easily spelled out analogy has made life insurance a great way to accomplish vital future income planning.

Point number two - According to Ellis, using a life insurance policy to assist in college planning is another idea whose time has come.

" The expense of college tuition is one of the most over-looked areas of financial planning today," said Ellis. "College planners are strongly warning parents to assemble a plan that will put their children through college without putting themselves into an impossible financial hole."

Ellis says that using life insurance as a tool for college funding allows parents to position their assets in a more favorable light in the eyes of the financial aid people. He says that even though people will often negotiate in buying a car and paying for a house, when it comes to a $350,000 price tag for college, people often don't use every option that is available to them.

New Long Term Care Provisions

Another aspect of life insurance that Ellis says few know about is the provision for long term care expense.

"Most people don't know that there are life insurance policies that have a hefty long term care provision built in, Ellis said. "Understanding and taking advantage of this simple provision can be the difference between keeping your savings or losing it all," he said.

Mr. Ellis went on to explain that one of the biggest pitfalls for retirees is not a sudden stock market reversal, but a financially devastating health care crisis.

"Nursing homes can cost in excess of $10,000 per month," said Ellis, "and with the average stay lasting 3.5 years, it's easy to see how a family could lose everything."

Ellis goes on to explain, "We are able to use saving account type vehicles that not only give a client 100% access to their funds at any point, but a significant long term care pool of benefits and a tax-free, probate-free, death benefit."

In the modern financial world, many are putting life insurance to work for them in a myriad of ways. It is proven to be a valuable tool for everything from estate planning to retirement income planning. The point of this message is to help educate individuals to the fact that, in the last few years, insurance companies have completely changed the format of their contracts to scratch America where it itches. If an insurance agent had gone to sleep like Rip Van Winkle in the 1960's and had awakened in this decade, he wouldn't recognize his chosen field of endeavor.

According to Ellis, the general public knows very little about the insurance they own. He says many are paying too much for the coverage they have.

"I offer free clinics where I have people come in and have their life insurance plans reviewed at no cost," Ellis said. "In nearly every case, those who attend discover they can either increase their coverage for the same amount, or keep what they have for less money." Those wishing more information may visit his webpage, www.shpfinancial.com.

CHAPTER SIX

Young People: Do What You Love; Love What You Do

"When I was 5 years old, my mother always told me that happiness was the key to life. When I went to school, they asked me what I wanted to be when I grew up. I wrote down 'happy.' They told me I didn't understand the assignment, and I told them they didn't understand life."

— John Lennon

One of the most valuable lessons I feel I can pass along to my children is this: In order to succeed in life, you should wake up every day and do something you love. Money will find you. You will find joy. Life will seem effortless.

During all of my working years, I have done just about every job imaginable. One job I had in my younger days was working on an assembly line at a candle factory in the Plymouth Industrial Park in Plymouth, Massachusetts. That was no party. I also worked in a warehouse where the temperature seemed like 200 degrees. My job involved shoveling horse manure in the stables that were situated behind the famous WPLM radio station in Plymouth. I can honestly say that each job, regardless of how hard the work was, was character- building.

My parents instilled in me a strong work ethic, too. My late father worked multiple jobs to keep food on the table and even took third shifts at various places of employment to pay for my expensive tuition at Sacred Heart High School. He kept this up through my college years to help pay for that expense. My mother toiled endlessly it seems, at all sorts of jobs, to help make ends meet. Somehow they kept the household afloat. If there were times when they did falter in that regard, they kept it from me. As a young kid, I never knew. But I never felt as if we were poor. To my recollection, I don't remember feeling deprived. I did sometimes wonder why the Easter bunny would bring the kid up the street a brand new bicycle, and I would get a package of Marshmallow Peeps and a hollow chocolate rabbit. That seemed to me to be a bit of a slight by the Easter bunny. However, in the end, I learned from my parents that work is called "work" for a reason. In the many arduous jobs that I would perform later in life, there were times when the work was so hard that I would become physically overwhelmed to the point that I learned just to put the body on autopilot, and would pace myself just so I could finish a shift. Time seemed to pass so slowly that I looked at the clock with disdain. The hours crawled by. Each minute seemed to last an eternity. But finally my 15-minute break would come. Now I could hang in there until my 30-minute lunch break, which would get me closer to home. In those days, I would get home so fatigued that, despite being so tired, I was reluctant to fall asleep because I knew the next sound I would hear would be the alarm, signaling me to do it all again.

Loving What You Do

Many of those with whom I have become acquainted as a financial planner have worked for 30 and 40 years at jobs they hated. I can understand staying the course when you have invested so many years into something that you feel like you cannot leave it. Sometimes money becomes the only incentive that keeps us at a job where we dislike the work and we dislike the people even more. Allow me to suggest that, for your own psychological well being, you find a way to either do something you love, or, failing that, find a way to fall in love with what you do.

Breaking away from a career that pays the bills just because you do not enjoy the work takes courage and a leap of faith, I know. I could tell you many stories about people who turned in their notice at their place of employment to begin a business, only to experience the heartache of seeing it fail. Failed restaurants are almost a proverb. There are stories to be told as well of individuals who were miserable at their jobs and, motivated by a book or lecture on positive thinking, simply decided one day that they would take their lemon and make lemonade with it. In other words, they made a decision to find reasons to love their work.

One individual I knew was a sales representative for a company that manufactured printing supplies. Business was off. He wasn't making his target quota. The boss was riding him constantly. He wanted to quit with every fiber in his being. But he couldn't leave because he needed he income and his retirement account was tied to his employer. He decided that he would find something he liked about every individual he worked with and every customer he called on. He would try to learn something new about that person each week. It wasn't long before he was happy in his job. Learning to love what he did for a living had a positive effect on his health. He began to sleep better. He started exercising and eating healthier foods. The positive thinking changed his life, he told me.

The Value of Saving

As parents, if we can teach our kids, both the youngsters and those of college age, the value of saving, we will have done them an immeasurably valuable service. A good rule to follow is what I call the "rule of thirds." After taking care of your immediate, essential expenses use the rest of the money as follows: a third goes into a savings account of some description; a third goes to indiscriminate spending as the kid sees fit (play money); a third goes to some form of charity.

This helps you accumulate money, enjoy the fruits of your hard work, and learn to help others. Once you are accustomed to that method of handling money you will be rich no matter how much you make. It will turn you into a successful person.

Look for a Career, Not a Job

So often, young people squander opportunities to build a successful working life because they settle for a job when they should search for a career opportunity. If you are a young person looking for a summer job, try to find one that is connected with the field you are considering as a career. I'm not talking about an internship, although that is a good idea. If you have a criminal justice major, for example, even working for a security company changing light bulbs can offer some excellent resume flair down the road. For all you education majors out there, working as an instructor at a summer camp can give your resume a great boost.

If you are in high school, such an entry on college application will let the admissions officers know that you are a person who values work and takes pride in accomplishment. Scholarships and grants may await you if you. That translates into money in your pocket. Let those who examine your college application know that you have the focus and drive to succeed. Show them that you are goal oriented and have a plan for the future. When I am in the position of hiring a young person to come to work for my organization, I look for those skill sets and attitudes. I know I am not the only one who does.

One of the best summers of my life was working as a counselor at Camp Bournedale in South Plymouth, Massachusetts. Not only did I stay in shape with constant activity like basketball, swimming, roller hockey and soccer, but I had three meals a day, a place to sleep and the networking opportunity of a lifetime.

The age in which we live seems dominated by social media. If you are a young person searching for that perfect summer job, post your wishes on Facebook, or whatever other networking site you feel is most popular at the time. You never know who might see your post and offer you the gig of a lifetime. While we are on the subject, a word of caution. If you are active on any of these social media sites, you can kill your chances of gaining the respect of those who may be in a position to hire you by indiscreet messages and inappropriate poses in photos. Once it's out there, it's out there. You can't un-ring a bell.

CHAPTER SEVEN
What Would I Tell Myself If Could Write a Letter to Me?

Letter to Me

If I could write a letter to me
And send it back in time to myself at seven-teen
First I'd prove it's me by sayin'
Look under your bed, there's a Skoal can and a Playboy
No one else would know you hid
And then I'd say I know it's tough
When you break up after seven months
And yeah I know you really liked her
And it just don't seem fair
But all I can say is pain like that is fast and it's rare

And oh you got so much goin' for you
Goin' right
But I know at seven-teen
It's hard to see past Friday night
She wasn't right for you
And still you feel like there's
A knife stickin' out of your back
And you're wonderin' if you'll survive

But you'll make it through this and you'll see
You're still around to write this letter to me

At the stop sign at Tomlinson and 8th
Always stop completely, don't just tap your brakes
And when you get a date with Bridgette
Make sure the tank is full
On second thought forget it, that one turns out kinda cool.
Each and every time you have a fight
Just assume you're wrong and daddy's right.
And you should really thank Miss Brinkman
She spent so much extra time
It's like she sees the diamond underneath
And she's polishin' you 'til you shine.

And oh you got so much goin' for you
Goin' right
But I know at seventeen
It's hard to see past Friday night
Tonight's the bonfire rally
But you're staying home instead
Because if you fail algebra
Mom and dad'll kill you dead
Trust me you'll squeak by and get a C
And you're still around to write this letter to me

You got so much up ahead
You'll make new friends
You should see your kids and wife
And I'd end by sayin' have no fear
These are nowhere near
The best years of your life

I guess I'll see you in the mirror
When you're a grown man

P.S. go hug aunt Rita every chance you can

And oh you got so much goin' for you
Goin' right
 But I know at seventeen
It's hard to see past Friday night
I wish you'd study Spanish
I wish you'd take a typing class
I wish you wouldn't worry let it be
I'd say have a little faith and you'll see

If I could write a letter to me
To me...

-Written by Brad Paisley

I am often asked what a young person can do to prepare for retirement, other than dumping every available extra penny into their 401(k) plans at work. It is so hard these days to save money, never mind have any type of estate plan or financial strategy. But this task should still be at the top of everyone's priority list.

If I could, in the words of my favorite country music artist Brad Paisley, "write a letter to me," that is send myself advice from today back to 1995 when I was 21 years old, it would include so much in the way of knowledge and information. The sad part of it is, I suppose, that it would still be ignored. But here it is anyway:

Invest in as many tax-free options as possible. A young person today should be concerned about what the tax rate will be when they get older and are ready to withdraw income from their 401(k), IRA, 403(b), or any tax qualified retirement account. Likely, it will be higher. For instance, if someone has dutifully saved $500,000 during the accumulation phase of their life, say for 30 years, and they are now looking to retire and live off of that nest egg, the true value of that account is only worth as much as the tax rate at the time of withdrawal.

If someone embarks on their savings future with the philosophy of taxing the "seed" rather than the "whole harvest", they will realize far more income down the road. Isn't that the point of saving for retirement anyway? Producing an income for our sunset years? It's easy to get caught up in the idea that socking away money on a tax-deferred basis today is the smart way to save. It is not necessarily so. Which makes more sense, paying taxes on the $400 that you put into your account today, at a rate we know, or waiting to pay taxes on $400,000 at an undetermined rate? The answer seems simple when put that way. Still, however, the most common way to save seems to be through the use of tax-deferred accounts, such as 401(k)s , IRAs and other places where the tax problem is only pushed off for a later time. The ironic part of this mindset is that most young people already have far more tax deductions and write-offs than they will have when they retire. Most likely, as they ease into retirement, the largest tax deduction, home mortgage interest, will be paid down considerably if not entirely paid off. That's less to write off. If they are self employed or own a business, and then retire, they will have fewer work-related deductions. If they raised a family, the kids leave home and can no longer be claimed as dependents.

Young people in particular could thrive on a concept which seems to be off the radar of many financial professionals – life insurance. Using a vehicle like life insurance is a long-term solution. First, a life insurance policy has a set benefit that will take care of your family obligations should you die. Second, any cash growth that occurs within the policy can be accessed tax free at any point throughout the owner's life.

The next logical question is, "How is a life insurance policy able to create growth? Over the last decade, new types of policies have appeared on the scene that offering the owner of the policy to have growth within their policy linked to a market index, such as the S&P 500, or the Dow. This means that your policy's cash value will accumulate based on the success of the market, but without any of the downside risk. It is this one new feature that makes policies so appealing, especially to the young and those in their middle years. Sure, you might get better numbers with a mutual fund or specific stock, but when you go to use it in the future you will be subject to the current value, either up or down, and the current tax rate. That spells a lot of uncertainty.

Another benefit to this type of planning is the ability to draw on the cash value of the policy to pay for life events. Where will the money come from when your daughter asks you to pay for her wedding? How about helping your children with college or buying their first home? What if an unforeseen legal or medical issue crops up that requires a lot of money in a short time? With traditional investments, an owner cannot touch the funds prior to their 59th birthday without incurring a big penalty PLUS the taxes. It would be far more efficient to have an account that would allow you to access your own money any time you want to, instead of when the government allows.

The current tax rate is at an all time historic low. Why doesn't it seem that way? Mainly because of who pays taxes and who does not. Despite the evidence that we see in the news every day about the national debt (which is at a whopping $15 trillion at the time of this writing), and Medicare & Medicaid dealing with the overwhelming influx of millions of new beneficiaries each year, and money troubles of the Social Security system, taxes still have remained relatively low. That is even stronger evidence that tax rates will be higher in the future.

Paying for College

Among the things that a young person needs to consider is obtaining a college education. Believe it or not, the tax-free plan mentioned above also has a credit savings plan that allows parents to not only save for their retirement, but also save for their children's college education – all with the same dollars!

Paying for a four-year college education here in the United States has become as expensive as buying a house. In some cases, one could purchase two family dwellings and one condo for what it cost to attend a four-year university and obtain a degree. It is to your advantage to sit down with a professional college planner so as to better understand the college funding "game." I refer to it as a game because there is much complexity involved in the process. Those who know how the process works can literally save thousands of dollars each year. Those who don't know the "rules of the game" will end up paying thousands of dollars extra. It is critical that you obtain an understanding the loan system, the process for applying for financial aid, and the forms that are required to apply for admission. It can be daunting and confusing. Have a professional help you with this and I promise it WILL save you lots and lots of money in the long run.

Dealing with Risk

The final step in my introductory course on what young people can do, is first understand risk and how to best utilize its benefits. Life is full of risks that you might not even know are there. There is an argument to be made that eliminating risk in a financial plan might suit an investor better in the long run than taking chances all of the time. There is the risk that your child will get accepted to Harvard University and you will need to come up with the $75K or so a year to pay for it. There is a risk that you might get into an accident and get sued for all of your assets. Then there are the risks that we can't even begin to assume that might get us on some random Wednesday afternoon.

Young people are often overlooked by a lot of the financial world mainly because they tend to have more debt than cash. So seeing that there is little opportunity to make significant money, they are not marketed to enough or encouraged enough to take the right steps.

CHAPTER EIGHT
You Don't Need a New Year To Make a Resolution!

"Don't say you don't have enough time. You have exactly the same number of hours per day that were given to Helen Keller, Pasteur, Michaelangelo, Mother Teresa, Leonardo da Vinci, Thomas Jefferson, and Albert Einstein."

— H. Jackson Brown Jr.

I have noticed that whenever the end of the year rolls around people begin asking me about year-end planning and what to do going into the new year. I'm not exactly sure if they are asking me to help them come up with their New Year's resolutions, but if that is the case, here it is: stop smoking (if you do), eat a bit less and take a jog once in a while.

As far as financial advice is concerned, it's 100% different - stop smoking, eat less and do a sit-up from time to time. Yes, that is sound financial advice, as you will see if you read to the end of the chapter.

During this new age of financial planning in which I have built my career, there has developed a definite link between your health and your wealth. This is especially true over the last decade. Good health can be a massive money saver for you and poor health can result in a disastrous drain on your savings. Yes, it is more expensive to eat better, shop organically and pay for gym memberships. But it is twice as expensive to pay 16 doctor co-pays per year, travel into the big city for specialist visits, and outfit your home with specially designed rails to assist you in and out the doors and up the stairs.

I have spent the last 10 years focusing on income planning for the conservative investor. People come to me because (a) they don't want to lose the money they have, and (b) they don't want to ever run out of money. Although sometimes I have been mistaken for Penn, of the comedy team Penn and Teller, I am neither a Las Vegas act nor am I a magician. I cannot create wealth where there isn't wealth, nor can I make it magically appear. Typically, once someone walks into my office they have already done all of the hard work. They are the ones who have sat in traffic for 35 years, saved their pennies, and taken care of their families. Once the client sits down with me in my conference room, they will usually have either one of two problems: Either they are going to die too soon, or they are going to live too long. Each is a scenario for which planning is needed.

Structured Settlements

As far as living too long, I think one of the most valuable things you can do to protect yourself against that, is securing a portion of your assets for guaranteed income later on down the road. Do not let that portion of your assets be at risk! It seems safe to say that the cost of everything will be greater in the future than it is today. That seems to be a given. The objective is to get as high a rate of return as possible without having the worry that your working assets could evaporate with a downward market swing. Structured Settlement Transfers have recently brought the investors into the modern era by allowing them to invest non-traditionally while getting traditional results. The average return on these investments is between 5% and 7%. As things improve in the marketplace, professionals who are familiar with these strategies expect those returns to go even higher.

Before you start slamming your fist on the coffee table shouting, "Scam!" or "Impossible!" keep in mind that a judge signs off on each of these investments in a court of law and the proceeds are paid to you by an A-rated financial institution. You can request a buyer's guide and list of sample cases by visiting www.shpfinancial.com. But before you do, ask yourself if you are doing everything in your power to make sure your money is working as hard as you did. Structured Settlement Transfers are short in supply, so there is a need to act quickly to take advantage of them. In essence, you are purchasing lottery or lawsuit payments from a seller who would like to secure a lump sum of cash right now.

Your Good Health Is Your Best Asset

Your health can also be a factor in whether or not your family has the ability to survive later in life. If you passed away at this very moment, what type of financial impact would your departure have on the people that mean the most to you? Does your pension end, or get reduced? How will your Social Security Payments be adjusted? What will your final expenses be? Will you leave behind a mound of medical bills to your spouse? No one knows what the future holds, so I always instruct clients to "control the things they can control and accept the things they cannot."

I think it is wise to accept the fact that our earthly departure is open ended. I think it is also wise to do what we can to stay here as long as possible. As far as I know, a brisk walk never killed anyone. No doctor that I know of has ever said to the surviving family members of a lost loved one, "If only he had walked less and eaten more butter, we would still be enjoying his company."

While you do your best to control your health through diet and exercise, accept the fact that things will happen that are simply beyond your control. Control that your money only goes up in value and not down, but accept the fact that you will never be able to die and have your bank account read "zero" on the same day. Control your assets with smart planning but accept the fact that outside forces can wreak havoc on your retirement if you let it.

In the months following the market crash of 2008, I grew very tired of hearing those who lost money in the downturn say that no one was immune to the disaster and that "everyone took a hit."

"I lost 60% of my 401(k)," I would hear, "but so did everyone else!" That statement was 1000% false! During that time, I was fortunate enough, with the company of my three other partners, to address a jam-packed room at the Plymouth Yacht Club in Plymouth, Massachusetts.

It was a client appreciation dinner and the room happened to be filled with individuals who had come through the worst free fall our market had experienced in many decades completely unscathed! My speech began with a declaration that not one person in this room had lost a dime in any of the market devaluation of the past eight months. Those words were followed by a five-minute ovation that brought goose bumps to all of us in the room, particularly me. It was a stark reminder to me of why I do what I do. Those people trusted us to do what we said we were going to do, and they were rewarded for having placed that trust in us. It is a sense of satisfaction I will never forget.

Another new year will be here before you know it. As it approaches, ask yourself how you can balance that ever-so-important three-legged retirement stool that symbolizes proper planning. The three legs are financial, legal and health planning. That will be the foundation holding you and your loved ones up. Don't neglect them. Do your sit-ups, update your legal documents, and review your financial plan to make sure you have a permanent future income

Make a New Year's DETERMINATION

This is for all those out there who have not planned for their financial future, or for those who need to review and update their financial plan. Regardless of what time of the year it happens to be when you read this, I want you to make a New Year's resolution. Yes, even if it is a hot day in the middle of summer, or a mild spring day in the merry, merry month of May, I want you to spend some time making a New Year's resolution. Why? Because, for some reason, when the ball drops on a new year, it is psychologically easier for us to forge a new beginning. So if that helps you slay the demons of procrastination and get to where you need to be in financial planning, then make it happen, Captain. This is your time.

When a new year is ushered in with all the fanfare and fireworks that accompany it, we can assume that most people will be making some personal promises to themselves. Usually, they revolve around some adjustment in their behavior that will make them a better version of themselves. They find the resetting of the calendar a great time to begin with a clean slate. Starting anew gives them new energy and drive to lose weight, eat better (or less), stop smoking, or just be kinder to their fellow man.

When it comes to physical fitness, it is interesting how full the parking lots of the local physical fitness gymnasiums are in the early days of January and how they begin to thin out toward the end of the month. That tells us that most resolutions aren't lived up to. So let's call it something else. If the semantics are useful in making it happen, let's call it a New Year's determination.

I have a front row seat for the passing of the financial parade, and I have come to the conclusion that the main reason people are reluctant to take steps to organize their financial affairs has to do with the perceived level of complexity they anticipate such an exercise will entail. People have a tendency to allocate time to the aspects of their life the way water runs down hill. It takes the course of least resistance. We are sometimes overwhelmed with obligations - both real and imagined - that must be attended to. We take them one at a time in the order of those that we feel can be quickly dispatched. That which nags at us the most is that which is taken care of soonest. Some may procrastinate going to the dentist until they feel the pain of the dreaded toothache. Others may wait until the day before the tax deadline to begin putting those papers together. It's human nature, I suppose. But let me ask you. Have you either set a budget or monitored your monthly expenses? Have you given any serious thought to your short term and long term financial goals? Have you looked at where you are in life now, and then envisioned where you will be financially in five years, 10 years, 15 years, 20 years and beyond. Have you outlined a path that will enable you to live a comfortable lifestyle when you arrive there?

If you haven't done any of those things, contact a professional for a checkup. I'm sure you believe it is prudent to have an annual physical examination, just as you believe it is wise to change the batteries on your home's smoke detectors. Taking care of your money should be just as important.

Some say, "I have nothing (or very little) to plan with, so why do I need to plan? I hear you. But that makes about as much sense to me as someone saying, "I have no energy and I'm having dizzy spells, so why do I need to see a doctor?" Assuming you are going to continue to be a viable member of society, have a job and pay taxes, if you have no plan and few assets, you are the prime candidate for seeing a financial professional and starting the planning process. It's never too late to start.

A few weeks ago, I explored the most valuable asset we all share here on planet Earth. No, not gold or stock in Apple, but something so pure and universal that no matter what your income level or lot in life, this one element tends to be sought after the most – time. Imagine being in the final days of your life, knowing that each second that passes is a lost treasure never to be recovered. What do you suppose people who know they are dying would ask for if given one wish? I suspect it would be for more time. More time to spend with loved ones. More time to experience the joy of life. More time to do more for others in the world. Sadly, only after we have lost a loved one do we hear the words, "I wish I could have spent one more day with my Dad." Or, "I wish I could have had one last conversation with my Mom."

Since you are making New Year's determinations, make it yours not to waste time. Do the financial, medical and legal things you need to do while you have the time. I have talked to several people who tell me that once those obligations are cared for, life's true sweetness can better be tasted like fine wine. You can swirl it, sniff it, sip it and swallow it down because the important things have been put aside and completed.

As I write this, I can't help but smile. I am doing what I love to do, using my education to teach others how to achieve their financial goals, and, happily, I am compensated for doing that which I love. For me, it is a pleasure coming to work and making a difference. Don't get me wrong. I enjoy my time off and the vacations I am privileged to spend with my wonderful family, but just knowing that when I blink awake in the morning that there are endless possibilities out there to be a positive influence in the lives of others makes for an exciting existence. I wish the same for you.

CHAPTER NINE

Seniors, Understand Your Health Options

"There's lots of people in this world who spend so much time watching their health that they haven't the time to enjoy it."

-Josh Billings

An often overlooked part of retirement planning is the cost of health insurance and the proper management of health-care expenses – in other words, facing down the innumerable choices for which the Medicare system allows. As a financial planner, I love options and choices. I pride myself on being able to present my clients with workable scenarios and viable options. But I am frustrated to no end when I see some of my clients sign up with the first health insurance option that comes along, when it's not the best choice for them. Sometimes ABC Insurance Company crosses their path at work. Or perhaps it was one a friend recommended. Either way, there are so many reasons why health coverage is not a one-size-fits-all decision. Making a snap decision here can cost seniors thousands of dollars.

Recently, I spoke with Matthew C. Peck of SHP Financial, who gave me the four fundamentals he teaches clients so as to help them make the best decision for themselves and their families.

1.) Location – Believe it or not, Medicare options are based on the county in which you live…not the state or region of the country. So, the coverage can vary wildly from one county to another. Plans available in two counties adjacent to each other may have different premiums. Or, one county may have a great plan available at a low premium and the neighboring county may not have it available. Unfortunately, this is not made altogether clear even in the Medicare & You book that comes out annually. It may change in the future, but at this writing, the government's guide displays the regional plans but is not county specific. If you are considering a specific plan, make sure it is available in your county and the premiums are what you thought they were.

2.) Doctors – Medicare plans break down into two separate and distinct categories: Medicare Advantage (MA) Plans and Medicare Supplement Plans. With Medicare Supplement plans, there is no network. You do not need to worry or ask your doctor if he or she accepts the Medicare Supplement Plan. It is the exact opposite when it comes to Medicare Advantage Plans. These less expensive plans (some are even zero-premium plans) subsidized by the federal government have networks. They are sometimes called PPOs or HMOs, or even HMO-POSs. If that sounds like alphabet soup to you, here are some definitions:

PPO - preferred provider organization (or sometimes referred to as a participating provider organization or preferred provider option) is a managed care organization of medical doctors, hospitals and other health-care providers who have covenanted with an insurer or a third-party administrator to provide health care at reduced rates to the insurer's or administrator's clients.

HMO - Health Maintenance Organization. Most Americans who have health insurance through their employer (and many who are self-insured or in Medicare Advantage Plans) have either an HMO or PPO. Usually, with an HMO, you choose a primary care physician who is your first contact for all medical care needs. The primary care physician provides general medical care and must be the one to refer you to a specialist. The most common types of managed care plans are health maintenance organizations (HMOs) and preferred provider organizations (PPOs). Less common are point-of-service (POS) plans that combine the features of an HMO and a PPO.

Before you enroll in a plan, make sure your doctor accepts the MA plan and is in the network. You could do the inverse of that by starting with your doctor. See what plan he or she accepts and whittle down your choices that way.

    3.) Health – Officially, brokers and insurance companies cannot 'cherry pick' whom they wish to insure. But you can. The rules vary state by state, but where I live, in Massachusetts, for example, there are no pre-existing conditions to enrollment. An exception is in the case of MA plans. They can exclude people with End State Renal Disease (ESRD). But basically, if your health starts to deteriorate, you can upgrade to the best plan available, one with no co-pays and deductibles, without an underwriting process or fear of rejection based on a health condition. In fact, on an annual basis during the Annual Enrollment Period, you can make that selection. By utilizing this choice, you can go with a less expensive plan with higher co-pays when you are younger and healthier, and then upgrade later in life, when health problems are more likely to occur. That will potentially save you thousands in premiums during the beginning and most active days of retirement.

    4.) Income – This is the most straightforward of the considerations. To spend $200 per month to one person might be a drop in the bucket, while $200 per month to another person could be one-fifth of their income. All of the factors above are good to keep in mind, but the bottom line is the same bottom line for everybody – cost. When considering all of your options, your income usually becomes the final arbiter in making choices regarding your health-care insurance in retirement, which is no surprise, really. It's that way with most life choices.

Is the Medicare system easy or consumer friendly? By no means! But seeking the guidance of an independent agent who is a trained professional, not a product pusher, can make the decision-making process a bit easier and enable you to more precisely manage your health care as a senior.

CHAPTER TEN

Who Should Consider a Reverse Mortgage?

"The question isn't at what age I want to retire, it's at what income."
-George Foreman

Recently I was talking to a client about issues pertaining to their situation and the topic of reverse mortgages came up. No sooner did I utter the "rev…" in "reverse mortgage," than both of my client's hands flew up to cover her ears like a nervous child about to be told they were getting punished. Over the past five years or so, the perception of what a reverse mortgage is and what it does has changed for the better in most people's eyes. But in light of my most recent experience, I felt it prudent to go over the basics once again. Please keep in mind that I do not sell reverse mortgages nor do I provide them at my firm. I do, however, believe that it is to everyone's benefit if the truth is clearly presented once and for all.

The first question in determining if a reverse mortgage is right for you or someone you know is to ask yourself, "Do I need or want any money at this stage of my life?" If the answer is "Yes" then the question becomes, "Where do I get the money?" Well, for people who own their homes, the answer might just lie in the next few paragraphs.

What Is A Reverse Mortgage?

A reverse mortgage is a loan designed for seniors, age 62 and older, which allows the borrower to get access to a portion of the equity in their home. There are no payments required by the lender for as long as the borrower is living in the home. The borrower is required to maintain the home, pay his or her property taxes and homeowner's insurance. The only time borrowers could be required to pay the loan back while living in the home is if they haven't paid their taxes and homeowner's insurance.

The reverse mortgage is insured by the Federal Housing Administration (FHA), which insures virtually all reverse mortgages through the Home Equity Conversion Mortgage program (HECM). When a borrower implements a reverse mortgage, the funds can be distributed as a lump sum, monthly payments, life payments or as a credit line. There are essentially two rate choices – fixed and adjustable. The fixed rate option requires the borrower to take all proceeds available as a lump sum. Typically, this will not make sense unless the borrower is using the funds to pay off a sizeable mortgage or unless the borrower has an immediate need for most or all of the funds. The adjustable rate option is more flexible as it offers all distribution options mentioned above. Most of the people I have seen take advantage of this program have done so to eliminate that big monthly mortgage payment that is cutsing into their cash flow. Just getting rid of that is, for a lot of people, like "found money" and is a big relief.

Even today, however, many misconceptions remain about reverse mortgages and how they work. Please let me dispel a few of them here. First, when you take a reverse mortgage you are not signing over title of your home to the bank. If I was doing my radio show on this topic, I would slowly repeat that for clarity and emphasis. A reverse mortgage is like any other mortgage in that respect. You still own your home.

What About Legacy?

Another myth I keep running into is the idea that you will leave your kids with nothing, or even potentially leave them with a big debt. While it is true that you are using some of the equity in your home, it is quite possible there will still be something left for your heirs at the end. How much equity will remain at the end of the line depends on how long you have the loan and on how much equity you drew down during the life of the loan. I often tell clients who use this reason as an excuse not to do a reverse mortgage that there are far more effective ways to leave wealth behind to children than inside the equity in your home. What if that was your plan in 2005 and you happened to die in 2010 when your equity may have diminished by 50%?

You can take some of the proceeds from the reverse mortgage and buy some life insurance where you could potentially leave double the original amount to your heirs and the amount you left would be both tax free and probate free. Furthermore, because the loan is insured by FHA, it's considered a non-recourse loan, which means neither you nor your estate can ever owe more than the value of the home. The only time the heirs would be responsible for a loan amount in excess of the value of the home is if they decided to keep the home. Otherwise, the insurance kicks in and makes everyone whole.

Closing costs for a reverse mortgage have historically been more than what you would pay for a traditional mortgage. The reason for the higher cost can be attributed to the insurance cost that accompanies all FHA-insured reverse mortgages. The borrower ultimately pays for the insurance in two forms: an upfront premium and an ongoing charge applied to your loan balance. It's the upfront premium that sometimes raises eyebrows. The one thing I kept coming back to in my research regarding the upfront closing costs is that virtually every penny is financed, and not out of pocket. This is important. Many people might shy away from looking at a reverse mortgage for fear that they don't have the money to cover the closing costs. It is still important to understand all the costs associated with this type of loan when determining if a reverse mortgage is the best option for you. Typically, the longer you plan to be in the home, the less expensive the upfront costs become on an annualized basis. In short, if you are looking for a short-term fix, then a reverse mortgage may not be for you.

The Saver Reverse Mortgage

In October 2010, FHA introduced the "Saver Reverse Mortgage," which, in many cases, can reduce the upfront costs by 50% to 60%, largely due to the minimal upfront insurance cost. From early indications, it looks like the Saver will appeal to a different type of reverse mortgage borrower.

According to Patrick Dougherty, head of the Reverse Mortgage Department at Coastal Finance, "It appears the Saver will be a good fit for those borrowers with higher priced homes with little or no mortgage balanceIn addition, the 'Saver' will probably be utilized more strategically by these borrowers. They will probably look to it as a cash flow tool to help prevent tapping investments or retirement assets that carry a tax liability every time you liquidate. In all honesty, the Saver may overtake traditional home equity loans & lines of credit, as it requires no monthly payments and does not require any income or minimum credit scores to qualify."

With that said, there are some tradeoffs when choosing the "Saver" over the standard reverse mortgage. First, the borrower will qualify for a lot less money with the "Saver," somewhere in the range of 20% to 25% less. Second, the interest rate for the "Saver" is typically higher than the standard. So, just because the loan costs less, it doesn't mean that it is right for everyone. It's important to speak with a reverse mortgage expert so they can explain both options to help you determine which one meets your needs and goals.

Who Should Look Into a Reverse Mortgage?

Who should be looking into a reverse mortgage? Well, my opinion is that anyone with any sort of cash flow issue, or someone who might be resisting spending money in retirement because of a fear of running out may be good candidates. I am a firm believer that, contrary to what Shirley MccLaine says about reincarnation, this is our one shot in this life. Let's enjoy ourselves. Reverse mortgages may be a good fit for folks who have a mortgage, but are having difficulty makings ends meet because their mortgage payment is punitive. When you implement the reverse mortgage, you essentially eliminate your monthly mortgage payment. For those seniors don't have a mortgage but live solely on Social Security and/or a pension, a reverse mortgage could possibly be an effective way to supplement their income, tax free.

Generally speaking, the reverse mortgage has helped countless seniors relieve financial stress by allowing borrowers to turn some of the equity in their home into cash so they can make repairs to their homes, help pay for ongoing maintenance, help pay rising tax bills, go on vacations or help pay for medical care. The list goes on and on, but according to Rob Kallagher from Ross Mortgage, "One of the most underrated benefits of a reverse mortgage is the stress it relieves related to not having enough money. I have had clients call me after their loan was closed crying with joy over how much the reverse mortgage improved their lives. I have to say that in my time in the financial services sector, I have never seen any financial product have such a profound and life changing impact on my clients. For the right people, a reverse mortgage can be excellent tool to help maintain or improve your lifestyle."

CHAPTER ELEVEN

Why There May Be A Financial Pot of Gold for Those Who Can Think Outside the Box

"Change your thoughts and you change your world."
-Norman Vincent Peale

Successful people share a common trait – they can think outside the box. They think differently, act differently and live their lives differently.

Recently, I had to do a little outside-the-box thinking when I was introduced to the concept of pre-owned annuities, or structured settlement transfers. I was introduced to the concept by my business partner, and one the Plymouth, Massachusetts area's smartest financial planners, Derek Gregoire. He telephoned me one sunny weekend afternoon to describe a conversation he had just had with an advisor friend we both knew in Los Angeles, California. I listened as Derek described this new financial instrument that would allow clients to have a safe place to park their money, for a predetermined period that could be as short as one year, or as long as 30 years, and receive a fixed rate of return of between 5% and 7%. Later, after we had done our due diligence on the product, we found that these financial instruments had a perfect track record for safety and that a judge in a court of law would even sign off on each one. But I must confess that my first reaction to it was negative. Why? Because, like most people, I was slow to think outside the box. I was also lazy. I was reluctant to put in the extra effort required to learn about something new. But then I thought of my own advice that I have been known to give out, about how people need to "get off their lazy rear ends" and get things done. I figured that I owed it to my clients, my family and my partners to dive into this new area of finance, and learn as much as possible. I began putting in the time to do just that, and what I found out was amazing. I knew it was an opportunity that I must tell my all my clients about as soon as possible.

The gist of the pre-owned annuities, or structured settlement transfers, can be summarized this way: There is someone out there who is currently receiving a payment from a structured settlement that was awarded to them by a decision in a court of law. Maybe they slipped and fell and won a lawsuit. Perhaps their coffee was too hot and they burned their lip. Maybe they were set to receive payments after a divorce decree. Regardless of the reason, they now want to sell off some of their future payments for a lump sum of cash now. When these individuals were initially awarded these payments, the judge assigned an A-rated insurance company to be the conduit for these payments. This way the plaintiff, or client, could have the assurance that their payment would arrive without fail, thanks to the financial security of the insurance company. By the way (or BTW, as my 12-year-old likes to say), the names of these insurance companies can be found in any major city in the United States on the sides of the tallest skyscrapers.

When the recipients of structured settlement payments sell all or part of their future periodic payments for a discounted present lump sum, the seller gets the cash, but the discount amount leas the door open for the investor to receive the future payments at a bargain. Here's an example:

An investor deposited $52,648 and received monthly payments of $2,590 from January 1, 2004 through December 1, 2008. The effective rate of return on this transaction was 7.5%. The investor received back $155,400 from the investment of $52,648. The company paying the checks has an A+ rating with A.M. Best and uses Snoopy in most of its commercials. This would be the perfect case for the person who is around 50 years of age, and who wants to secure five years worth of income when they turn 65. I'm going to go ahead and say it. There is no way you are going to find a straight up 7.5% return on your money like that anywhere else.

Here's another case. My client puts in $38,732 today, and receives $105,000 in return from an A+ rated company in the form of payments consisting of three lump sums - $60,000, $30,000 and $15,000, over a period of 25 years or so. The total rate of return would be approximately 7.25 %.

But every opportunity has a downside. So what is the downside to this investment opportunity? First, each case that is presented is only available for a single person to buy. Just like a house on the market or a car advertised for sale, only one buyer can purchase each case . There is a waiting list for these structured settlement transfers and the investor who wishes to participate needs to act quickly. You must have the cell phone number of the advisor dealing with these, because they are only available for a short time. You have to be ready to go when the bell rings.

Secondly, once your participation in a settlement transfer is official, it cannot be changed. As soon as the judge signs off on the case, and you legally become the owner of those payments, it takes an act of God to resell or make changes. So it is vital that you know for sure that you have all of your questions answered, know these products inside and out, and are comfortable with the transaction.

Thirdly, since we are dealing with the court system, there can be delays. To compensate, we have learned to factor the delays into our expectations. We figure that it will take approximately three months from start to finish. Investors have told me that they didn't mind the slight inconvenience in view of the benefits they experienced. A case could be also denied by a judge because of incomplete information from the seller, payments that don't really exist, or a general impression on the part of the judge that the transfer isn't in the best interest of all the parties involved.

One final characteristic of this type of transaction that may be considered a downside could also be one of its strong points – interest rate fluctuation. Those rates of 5% to 7% are solid as I write this. Actually they are pretty astounding! But what will the interest rate environment look like in five years, 10 years, or 20 years? If you are of the school of thought that interest rates are on the rise right now, then a shorter-term deal might be more palatable. But, if you think as do I, that it will be a long time before rates start to recover, then looking one to 15 years out isn't so bad. Those rates are set and locked in. No changing. No sir. No how.

CHAPTER TWELVE

How Do We Protect Our Most Valuable Assets?

"Life is an opportunity, benefit from it.
Life is beauty, admire it.
Life is a dream, realize it.
Life is a challenge, meet it.
Life is a duty, complete it.
Life is a game, play it.
Life is a promise, fulfill it.
Life is sorrow, overcome it.
Life is a song, sing it.
Life is a struggle, accept it.
Life is a tragedy, confront it.
Life is an adventure, dare it.
Life is luck, make it.
Life is too precious, do not destroy it.
Life is life, fight for it."

— Mother Teresa

What does the concept of "asset protection" really mean? I use it every day when I introduce myself to a new client. When I go on the air for my radio and TV programs, I throw out the term "asset protection" liberally because it is in large measure the function my company provides. I also use the phrase "asset protection" daily in commercials. But what does it really mean?

Many of the conversations I have with people I meet go something like this:

"I specialize in asset protection…"

"I have no assets worth protecting..."

"Really?"

"Not a thing! But when I do get something I'll give you a call."

"Great, here is my card."

As you can see, it leaves no room for discussion when people believe they have nothing in their lives worth protecting. Here's where I feel the modern age of financial planning and "asset protection" needs a good, old-fashioned makeover.

Assets are possessions. Society has somehow come to think of assets as stocks and bonds, property, antiques, automobiles or money. But to identify what your assets are, simply ask one simple question – What do you value the most? When that question is answered with honesty and thought, the results will be most revealing. We will most assuredly list such things as family, spirituality, health, country and friendship. You probably won't see "money" at the top of the list, if it makes the list at all.

If there is a fire in your home, will you grab the deed to your time-share during your escape, or will you rescue your loved ones? I ask a lot of people what they have done to protect their assets, and their minds go immediately to money, property, insurance and legal documents. However, those are basically just the tools, or mechanisms, we use in protecting the things we really cherish and value in our lives.

In the columns I write week after week, I make mention of ways we can all help fund our retirement, get legal help, buy insurance and use other financial strategies. But in the end, protecting our assets is the most important topic I could possibly cover because it deals with what we treasure and cherish. Of course, this is different for everyone.

Our Most Valuable Assets

To me, family is number one. My health, country, town and friendships are close behind. Earlier I mentioned spirituality. This is an asset I have but one that I seem to always need to work on and replenish. It is like fine silver that seems to be always in need of polishing. Spirituality is the inner mystery that keeps us balanced. Ideally, this sense of spirituality should be what protects us when things look grim, when times are tough or when logic cannot provide an answer to troubles that blindside us from time to time. Lately, the media appear to be waging a war against spirituality for reasons I cannot quite fathom. And somehow, our culture has decided this asset isn't worth protecting. Yet with all of that working against it, the idea of spirituality remains strong. Churches remained filled with people looking to protect that most cherished asset. Do we visit our bank every week to pray over our accounts and give thanks for our CD rates? No. But when you ask people to list their assets, the bank account shows up but their faith is not mentioned.

Time - A Most Valuable Asset

During a recent Thanksgiving, I remember thinking that we thank God for lots of things – our family, friends and our lives. We should also thank him, I believe, for the gift of time. Each moment we have presently is a gift. Each moment we have the promise of in the future is a gift. Each moment we can remember from our past is a gift.

In finance, time is one of the most salient factors in building wealth. Even if rates on CDs were at 10% right now, and if you only had your money there for three weeks, you would not really benefit. I call it "Time Value of Money," or TVM. The rate is only as good as the time you have it invested. Time and interest are just like a married couple. When things are good, like when you are saving, the two perform like a well-oiled machine, providing consistent results that can produce a long-term benefit and a happy retirement. When things are bad, like when you owe money, the time and interest can act like a miserable couple, where every day, things get worse, with less and less of a chance the relationship will reconcile.

Here is a case in point: Is 20% a good figure, or a bad figure? I suppose it depends if it's a happy marriage or bad one. If you owe 20% on a mortgage or credit card, I would hope you would want time and interest to file for a divorce as quickly as possible! However, if your CD was somehow paying that, it would be a loving relationship from here to eternity!

I recently met with a couple in their early 50s. They were interested in the "pension review" they heard me discuss on my weekend radio program. To them, time played a pivotal role in how they viewed their current situation. I told them that right now, the marketplace has income plans that allow for people to double their money in a 10-year period, guaranteed. This marriage of time and interest became the perfect solution to a question that had haunted them over the past few years, "How much money will we have for income once we retire?"

Will I Run Out of Money?

Another common question people have is, "Will we have enough money to retire?" Then the biggie...the fear of all fears..."Will I run out of money in my old age?" For this 50-something couple, time and interest were vital to them reaching all of their goals.

Time is indeed a precious commodity when it comes to retirement planning. We all know compounding is good. But just how good it is may shock you. EXAMPLE: Beth is 21 years old. If Beth places $5,000 into a Roth IRA, never adds a cent to it, and gets an 8% return compounded, when she is 66 years old the IRA will be worth $160,000.

I can hear the question forming already, "How is Beth supposed to get 8% over that time frame?"

No, I'm not crazy. Yes, I do follow the regular postings of interest rates of banks, investment firms and insurance companies. But the truth is, anyone who has read my articles in the print media and heard my comments on radio and television, knows I have, on several occasions, explained how structured settlement transfers work and how that they are a guaranteed way to accomplish just that type of scenario. If Beth has the right guidance or assistance from, say, a parent or grandparent, she can certainly reach, accomplish and achieve these goals! Now if Beth decides to wait until she is 39 to start with this investment, the results at 66 will only generate a value of $40,000. That demonstrates the power of compounding interest.

So often, clients ask about leaving money behind in their estate for the benefit of their children and grandchildren. Usually, these clients have the same thing in mind – college tuition accounts for the grandkids and a CD or two for their grown ones. That is what they ask for, and what I offer them is a whole other thing!

Mr. and Mrs. Jones were each 69 years old and together they had over $300,000 in savings and CDs that were earning nearly nothing. Their income was set. They had pensions through their former employers (rapidly becoming a thing of the past) and Social Security. The couple had a home paid for in full and two IRAs worth $150,000. They wanted to leave $100,000 behind to their four grandchildren to use for college. If they went ahead with their self-created plan, their $100,000 would only be worth $150,000 by the time the kids entered college. Given the cost of a college education these days that may sound like a lot, but it is not.

They placed $116,314.52 in a structured settlement transfer case and, by court order, will leave behind $1,000,000 to their grandchildren when they reach the ages of 38, 41, 44 and 49! (The grandchildren are young now). With this program, there is no health underwriting, no winks of "projected" or "possible" results, only pure, court-ordered guarantees! In essence, the grandparents gave time and interest as a gift. The investment grows at 7.5% and pays off during a time when the money can come in the most handy. What 40-something person with kids, a job, a mortgage and bills out the wazoo could not use $250,000?

Another client took the opportunity to invest $40,225 into a structured settlement paying 7.5% as well. This was to give each of their grandkids a $45,000 check on August 4, 2008, and another for $180,000 on August 4, 2038. Once again, the checks would come from an A+ rated financial institution, guaranteed and court ordered.

CHAPTER THIRTEEN

Paying our Fair Share of Taxes Doesn't Mean Paying More

"We contend that for a nation to try to tax itself into prosperity is like a man standing in a bucket and trying to lift himself up by the handle."

-Sir Winston Churchill

Paying taxes, according to some politicians, is a citizen's proud and patriotic duty. I'm as patriotic as the next guy, I assure you. And I pay my taxes. What I do not like is paying more than my fair share.

According to some statistics I've seen, half the population of the country pays no income tax at all. I wonder if these politicians realize that. I suppose that makes those people who don't pay taxes unpatriotic. I recently heard a promise made by those capable of making policy in this regard that taxes would be increased, but not on families earning less than $250,000 per year. What made that promise so brilliant is that to keep it, all you have to do is change the word "taxes" to "fees" and hope the public is too stupid to figure it out.

If you increase taxes on businesses, from whom does that tax increase ultimately come? Tax increases to businesses are, of course, passed along to the consumer. Banks are an excellent example of how the government, by its unwarranted involvement in the free enterprise system, ends up crushing the consumer. CD rates, low to begin with, had the placed upon them the additional cost of an increased Federal Deposit Insurance Corporation (FDIC) premium hike. This was due to the limit increases applied a few years previously, forcing banks to insure $250,000 per account instead of the previous limit of $100,000. This additional protection for the consumer came at a price, however. This one public relations move on the part of government created a whole new conundrum for the conservative investor: Do I worry about my bank going under or about my principle evaporating from inflation and low interest? FDIC coverage also discourages the public from looking at bank ratings or their financial health. "Why worry, if it's all guaranteed by the government?" they reason.

The FDIC isn't the only culprit in keeping bank rates low and fees high. In 2001, the International Money Laundering Abatement and Financial Anti-Terrorism Act hit the banking world. This legislation required banks to keep additional records relating to suspicious banking. This, in turn, required them to increase staff to accommodate the new law and train staff members on the new measures. In addition, there was the need to develop new and advanced communication channels between government agencies and the banks. Was the program worthwhile and did it serve a useful purpose? Yes. But that isn't the point being made here. Public safety and consumer protection are always important. I'm just pointing out the many costs associated with banking that the public in general is completely unaware of. But there has been a revival of consumer interest where our tiny voices are being heard.

HR 4646

Bank of America recently rescinded plans to impose certain fees on customers because of public outcry. As this is being written, a path has been laid for us to knock down this next government fee – HR 4646, a bill being recommended that will impose a 1% tax on all transactions at any financial institution, credit union, bank and savings and loan. I know, 1% doesn't sound like much, so why get all worked up about it? Well, this tax also applies to ALL direct deposit transactions such as pension checks, Social Security checks and tax returns. If my math is correct, you will shell out $10 just to have a $1,000 check clear. So the end around is to hand deliver the check and avoid that silly tax, right? Sorry, even a normal deposit faces that tax.

As I was writing the above information, I began to get a bit dizzy. I figured that this couldn't possibly be something that our elected officials were really considering. I had to be missing something I literally left my computer, walked around, made some calls and found out that not only is it true, but there is video footage of what is called the "Transaction Tax" being discussed. You may check it out yourself by visiting the following website: www.tinyurl.com/24dn5ud and checking out the article and video clip that appears under the heading, "Transaction Tax Has 'a Great Deal of Merit'." The video is from 2009, but as of this writing, the proposition is still on the table. Hopefully it has no chance of becoming law. But it is clear that the public who votes law makers into congress may have little knowledge of what they are actually up to until it's too late. If video clips like that were broadcast during American Idol, public awareness would be heightened, I'm sure.

I'm not trying to stir up a contentious political debate here; I just want people to take some responsibility for what happens to us and do something about it. It would be healthier for the country if this could be done before we actually send some of these people to Washington. When it comes to health care, banking, taxes, public programs and the like, we need to ask the question, "Who is paying the tab?" If your answer is "them" or "the government," then you most likely are not a taxpayer and enjoy taking more than giving. If you answered "us," then you recognize that taxes come from our paychecks, tolls, fees, property taxes, excise taxes, local sales taxes, automobile inspection sticker fees, gasoline taxes, estate taxes, probate costs and the list goes on and on.

In other words, the money comes from us. It appears to me we have a problem to fix both in our own homes and in Washington. Increasing the bill for the middle class isn't the answer. Demonizing the wealthy for success isn't the answer either. We all need to chip in and do our fair share to pull the country forward. You are either a puller or someone being pulled. Being pulled isn't a bad thing. But if times are tough and you are down and out, then get your rest by letting your brothers and sisters help you out. But once you catch your breath, then get back into harness and begin pulling again so others can breathe. We print "We the people" on our money. We chisel "We the people" on granite portico entryways to our museums and courthouses. We read it embossed on all things American and hear it repeated anytime anything American is celebrated. Yet many still think of a government handout as "free money."

The next time April 15 rolls around, pretend you have a choice. Pretend you can decide on what you would pay in the way of taxes, and then vote with that mindset. If only half of us did that, then we might get a bit more respect from those who think it fine with us if they have their hands buried in our pockets.

CHAPTER FOURTEEN
It's Time to Start Putting the US Back in the USA

"The cement of this union is the heart-blood of every American."
-Thomas Jefferson

I think I am like most people in the sense that I dislike negative political ads. I feel as if someone is trying to manipulate me by force-feeding me lies. I dislike the lies, manipulation and the twisting that goes on during political campaigns. In fact, if I could avoid all of it, I would. If it didn't mean so much to have the right person in office, both locally and nationally, I would just continue my normal routine of watching re-runs of The Office and eating junk food, while staying clear of political elections and all the dirty games that seem to accompany them. But politics is essential to the well-being of the country. So non-involvement is just not an option.

My profession deals directly with the protection of my clients' assets and preserving their wealth for a healthy and happy retirement. Most of the people who walk into my office are hard-working, blue-collar folks who did everything by the book, and did it with honor. All they ask is that they be allowed to keep what they saved and protect their nest egg from being fleeced. So my choice is always for less government rather than more.

Shrinking Big Government

The story is told of a Republican and Democrat who were walking down a city street together one afternoon. They both came across a homeless man who asked for some assistance. The Republican and Democrat look at each other and both agreed to help the man out. The Republican reaches into his pocket and pulls out a $10 bill and hands it to the homeless man. The Democrat reaches into the Republican's pocket and pulls out a $10 bill and gives it to the homeless man.

I love that story. It is a splendid example of how big government tends to behave. It is way too bulky and is so often misused. At its roots, the Republican Party seems to be dedicated to the task of shrinking the role of government in our lives, which is why they are sometimes unfairly called greedy, insensitive, racist and other negatives. The assumption is that the government is the only viable source of assistance and charity in the United States, when the truth is that most charitable giving comes from the country's large corporations and institutions that, somewhere along the line, have been castigated as villains and thieves. These corporations are the target of the "Occupy" movement. They are in the protesters' crosshairs because, to quote the ones carrying signs and bullhorns, they think of nothing but profits and they are evil because they don't hire people and lend money. How ironic is that?

Does greed, evil and selfishness run in the veins and hearts of some of the bigger companies in the United States? To be sure, they do. But to blanket the entire Fortune 500 as rotten is not only incorrect, but I believe harmful to the very spirit that made America what it is today.

Our children deserve to live out the American dream and see it is real. Sadly, we are taking that away from them, not with less opportunity but with political correctness run amok. We have taught them that struggling is the product of someone else taking what is yours. We have instilled in them the notion that it is someone else who caused their misfortune and that "others" are keeping them down. We are not teaching them how to rise and overcome the challenges life presents.

Elections are not about Republicans and Democrats. They are about deciding what the role of government is and what we need to do as citizens to move it forward. Personally, I will vote for anyone who is willing to shrink down the size of big government, reduce our taxes and keep government out of the way of progress. Living in the state of Massachusetts, I naturally follow the career of New England Patriots quarterback Tom Brady. He throws the ball with the velocity and accuracy of Pathfinder guided missile. But how effective would he be if, at the beginning of each game, he had to be handicapped by having a 10-pound weight strapped to his right arm? That is what government is doing to small businesses these days. If you own a business, you are handicapped by needless and unfair regulation, unusually high taxes, exorbitant fees and endless red tape. It is enough to discourage any private citizen from creating new enterprise. Ideas are lost in piles of paperwork and forms. Instead of coaching new enterprise, big government seems to be playing defense against it.

As a business owner, I will show up at work each day with the fight in my heart. I will hire and create and hopefully succeed. Those who think like me refuse to blame things on "hard times." As I wrote earlier, if times are hard, then more work is required. It is my belief our government should protect us like a shield. We are on offense, striving for progress. Our government should be on our team, leading the way, not playing for the opposition, like a bunch of linebackers trying to swat down our passes. I think that's what it's all about...putting the US back in the USA.

Corporation Bashing

It has become popular these days for folks who are disenchanted with their lot in life to bash corporate America for all the ills that plague our nation. Corporation CEOs are an easy target. These are people you wouldn't recognize if you saw them on the street or in a park. An average citizen couldn't pick them out of a lineup. But these folks have been castigated as heartless demons and are expected to absorb the brunt of the anger that seems to be permeating the nation as this book is written. Think of what the public has been debating over the last few years. During the last presidential election, each candidate accused the other one of "being friends with the oil industry," as if this were somehow scandalous. Neither candidate rose to defend corporate America for all that is good about it for fear the media would vilify them with the same disdain as they do those they call "the wealthy," as if that were some sort of crime too.

We now have a term called the one percent. Do I even need to explain what that is? Just hearing that conjures up negative thoughts of evil Gordon Gekko-like figures who do nothing but kill babies and count money. The truth is that demonizing the wealthy is the product of an ugly personality trait that humans sometimes display to deflect their own shortcomings. I am in no way defending the one percent of the most wealthy Americans nor am I implying that they are all great human beings. My point is to merely point out that we are focusing on the wrong issues.

The Buffet Rule

According to the Tax Policy Center, the Buffett Rule would bring in about $20 billion per year. The Buffet rule is a tax plan proposed by President Barack Obama in 2011 that would apply a minimum tax rate of 30% on individuals earning more than a million dollars a year. The Buffett Rule is named after American investor Warren Buffett who publicly stated in early 2011 that he disagreed with idea that rich people, like himself, should pay less in federal taxes, as a portion of income, than the middle class. The rule would implement a higher minimum tax rate for taxpayers in the highest income bracket to ensure they do not pay a lower percentage of income in taxes than less-affluent Americans. According to a White House official, the new tax rate would impact 0.3 percent of all taxpayers.

The $20 billion makes up only about 3% of the overall deficit, so one wonders why so many are giving this tax issue 100% of their attention? I recently had the privilege to hear a lecture from the former head of the Government Accountability Office, David Walker. In his book, Comeback America, Walker detailed how to get the nation back on track before it is too late. "What is scary," he said, "is that we are on the brink of reaching a "tipping point" where 51% of the country is paying no taxes and is totally dependent on the government for their daily needs."

According to Walker, once we reach that point, we will essentially be like an out-of-control boulder thundering down a mountain and over a cliff. The "tipping point" makes those who are dependent on the government for their support a voting majority. Walker discussed the need to reform Medicare, Social Security and other programs that are taken advantage of and are either operating in the red or running out of money. He pointed out that reforming these programs would be painful to many who have become dependent upon them, and the subject of doing so has become a political land mine that most candidates for office try to steer clear of. I agree with Walker, that tough times call for tough actions. Tough actions require tough leaders. If nothing at all is done, the entire system will collapse, plain and simple.

Walker served as United States Comptroller General from 1998 to 2008, and is Founder and CEO of the Comeback America Initiative.

Tax Reform

Tax reform is the real issue. Directing our attention to the Buffet Rule is lazy and pointless and merely an act of pandering that is intended to get votes. Who can we point fingers at other than ourselves? What needs to happen is that the system needs to be fixed, and every American man, woman and child needs to have skin in the game. Isn't that what our nation is about? Does the expression "We the People" mean anything anymore, or is it time we change it up to "Some other people," or "Those people over there."

Federal Reserve Chairman Ben Bernanke, testifying on June 7, 2012, before the Joint Economic Committee of Congress, said that if nothing is done about the Bush Tax cuts expiring at the end of 2012, then we are in for a world recession that would affect all of us, not just the 1% of Americans referred to as the upper class. Yet the media, the general public and the anti-Bush crowd wants us all to believe the tax cuts were just for the rich and wealthy.

How about this: As it stands right now, with no action taken by Washington, American taxpayers will be shelling out $310 billion more next year. Not to mention that unemployment will continue to grow and companies will seek global solutions to our national tax problem. The expression "global solutions" is another way of saying outsourcing jobs. Not high-paying 1% jobs, but middle-class production jobs, factory jobs, manufacturing jobs. The kind of nine-to-five jobs at which we ordinary Americans work. The kind of jobs you hear about in country songs written by Toby Keith, where you bust your rear end all day, and then go toss a beer down on Friday night as a reward for earning a paycheck.

The finger-pointing and partisan politics need to cease. If you think tax increases are the way to fix the problem, then consider how a smaller paycheck will help incentivize you to buy more in the community.

Like it or not, the economy is fueled by businessmen and women, big and small, who build things, sell things and offer the public stuff they want to buy. If they offer something that the public doesn't want, then they don't sell anything and they go broke. The government's public relations firm has persuaded us to believe that what's wrong with our society starts and ends with the people who are making the money. It has become a dirty thing to make money, yet we all try our hardest to do it. This deadly sin, jealousy, has manipulated us to yell out, "You make too much money!" We don't do that with other successes. "Hey, you! You lost too much weight. You need to share your weight loss with other people who can't lose weight!" Or "Your grades are too good! It's not fair, give half of it back to the kids who didn't get good marks." It sounds utterly ridiculous when we phrase it like that, but with money it is par for the course.

The government is now using taxes as a way of policing what we should and shouldn't do. Taxing cigarettes, alcohol and "behaviors" are totally acceptable because we can demonize those things. Therefore, the folks who use those items responsibly and in an appropriate way are still taxed because they are deemed "bad."

It all comes down to personal responsibility. Everyone needs to row the boat in order for it to glide smoothly through the waters of history. Europe failed at this and so will we if we aren't careful. David Walker believes that restoring our nation begins and ends with responsible people making tough decisions. Will that happen? We can either wait and see, or try to make changes now.

CHAPTER FIFTEEN

Open Letter to the President

"Each man must for himself alone decide what is right and what is wrong, which course is patriotic and which isn't. You cannot shirk this and be a man. To decide against your conviction is to be an unqualified and excusable traitor, both to yourself and to your country, let men label you as they may." -Mark Twain

From: Chuck Nilosek
To: The President of the United States

Dear Mr. President,
 I hope all is well with you and your family there in Washington, D.C., and I thank you for taking the time to read this letter. I just want to make a few suggestions on how we can improve things a little bit in America. I know you're aware of some of the problems we have been having lately.
 I know that you are crazy busy there, but we really need to do something about the jobs issue. I'm talking about unemployment, Mr. President. No offense, but I hear a lot of speeches come out of Washington but most of it appears to me to be just so much political rhetoric. Everyone gets emotionally charged up when they hear slogans, like "Let's get America

back to work," but I'm not sure what that means. I don't think a lot of other people are, either.

If you don't mind taking a little bit of advice from someone as ordinary as me, I think you might discover there are some pretty basic things we can do as a nation to get back on track. First of all, I have been reading a lot of articles lately on how we can encourage businesses to bring some of their money and manufacturing back to our country. I'm sure that I am not telling you anything you don't already know, Mr. President, but the corporate tax rate at 35% is way too high, and with over a trillion dollars sitting outside of our country just begging to come home, I think that it could be lowered to, say 20%. I promise you a lot of that money would come back home. Then that tax benefit could be increased to 22.9%, still keeping it less than Europe's, and it would give these corporations great incentive to stay here by creating some tax certainty.

Mr. President, I heard that if Japan lowers their corporate tax rate a bit, it will officially make the United States the most expensive place in the world to do business. I am not blaming you for this, Mr. President. I know it was this way before you were elected Commander in Chief. But if we want to "get America back to work," then we need to have a place of business for these workers to go, right?

I also read where one think tank called the Cato Institute estimated this action would create 350,000 more manufacturing jobs by the year 2019. The ripple effect would then lead to more than 1.7 million more jobs. Wouldn't that be great for America – to see the country bracing for hundreds of new factories? Just think – all of this because of our government's friendly invitation to come here and set up shop. I feel a little silly just bringing this up. I'm sure you are working on it right now. But just in case you are not, establishing a policy like that would kill two birds with one stone. It would reduce the unemployment rate while at the same time bring in additional tax dollars that can go toward cutting the deficit a bit.

By the way, I love the idea about pumping more stimulus money into the economy by building more bridges and tunnels and improving our nation's highway system. That might even make our work commutes shorter. But what is the point if we have nowhere to commute to? What will the trucks be delivering if everything is made overseas. I see your point –

more government jobs and more people dependent on the government intravenous drip of federal aid. But we might need to call an audible on that one, Mr. President.

If you are still reading, sir, I would also like to propose a plan to require every citizen here in the U.S. to pay their fair share of taxes. I did a little non-scientific survey of the people in my car today and found that 100% of the people polled agree that the IRS tax code needs to be reformed and simplified. Why? Mainly because the forms are beyond comprehension to the average Joe, and people have no idea what they are paying and why. Do you think this is why so many have lost a sense of ownership in the operation of our government? Just this week I paid for an inspection sticker, an excise tax and a license fee just to operate my business here in Massachusetts. I also pay hundreds of dollars a year in tolls to collect funds to pay for a road that has already been paid for, not to mention the sales tax on all the items I purchase on a daily basis. I pay $1,600 per month on health insurance and still have to pay when I walk into the emergency room. Mr. President, as you can see by the outrage of the members of the Tea Party and others who are fed up, the people in the middle class feel as if they are the ones getting the worst of the storm. Just as we need to go after the mega rich in this country and make them pay their fair share, we need to go to the people who don't work, or have anything, and make them contribute something for the services they use.

Mr. President, I know for a fact most people feel helpless and lost when they are totally dependent on the government for their existence. Most of those people, I hope, would want to earn their keep with some type of work to justify getting a government handout. Wouldn't it be wonderful to replace welfare with paychecks? We could give businesses a big, big tax incentive to hire folks to do temporary work until they can get back on their feet and find something permanent. Can you imagine the overwhelming feeling of accomplishment these people would have after finishing up a hard day of work? I'm sure it's the same way you and I feel, sir.

Then, we need to close up loopholes for the other end of the spectrum. We hear of tales of corporate executives paying less in taxes than secretaries that answer their phones. Although a complete tax overhaul would put a lot of tax professionals out of business, it would go a long way in building up our sense of national pride and true ownership in the ol' red, white and blue. It has seemed to me, Mr. President, that a lot of the people who are paying taxes feel it's a case of 'us versus them,' instead of 'us united.' I would be happy to pay my fair share when I know it is going to schools, fire fighters, military and public safety. I don't, however, like it when I hear my money goes to things that are controversial, or against the moral fabric of the country. If we keep it simple, we will have more success. Do you think the complexity of our system of government is intentional, perhaps designed to distract us so Washington can take our money and waste it on things that, if put it to a vote, would never have a chance?

Mr. President, government waste and fraud is another huge issue. Can you imagine how much change we could find in the cushions of the sofa just by eliminating waste? As you know, the future of this nation rests in its citizens. These are the ordinary folks who will create companies large and small. They are the ones who will invent the latest technology, cure diseases, solve the hunger problem and help their neighbors. They are the answer to the energy crisis. They are the solution to the progress that would be made were it not for the regulatory roadblocks that stand defiantly in the way. These roadblocks need to be removed, Mr. President. Government needs to get out of the way and allow the process of capitalism to flow unobstructed though the veins of our nation. Allow that to happen and you will see the color return to the stars and stripes. If a business can operate without the worry of roadblocks likes excessive permits holdups, license delays and suffocating fees and taxes, then development would flourish.

I know what you are thinking, Mr. President. If we corporate fat cats run amok without government oversight, then it will create an atmosphere of total anarchy. But the people of this country are the best in the world at everything and we need to get back to proving it. I am not alone, Mr. President. I am not a voice in the wilderness. There is a multitude of people who think as I do. If you don't believe me, just check out route 128 here in Massachusetts every day at 7 a.m. Those people are going to work. Half their week is spent paying taxes, and the other half goes to feeding their families. Many of them still have your bumper stickers on their cars. They are willing to vote for you again if you can turn things around.

In closing, Mr. President, I know you are very concerned and interested in Wall Street too. I have heard your speeches on that very topic. So here is my biggest tip of the day. Are you ready? If you let those companies that make up the DOW Jones, S&P 500 and the NASDAQ thrive, then the people who work for them will thrive. Their 401(k) accounts will thrive. My IRA will allow me to be less dependent on Social Security and Medicaid. You will get the credit for a bull market and people will hire. I know you want to help and God bless you for it. But you need to let us do our thing. We might fall a few times and skin our knees, but we will rebound. But if you hover over us, like those crazy helicopter moms at the park, we will never learn how to behave on our own. I know you care and love us, but let us live. Let us spread our wings and fly. Thank you, Mr. President, for reading this, and I hope we can move ahead.

Respectfully, your fellow American,
Chuck Nilosek

CHAPTER SIXTEEN
Control What You Can; Accept What You Can't Control

"I do not want to foresee the future. I am concerned with taking care of the present. God has given me no control over the moment following."

-Mahatma Gandhi

As most of my close friends know, I hate the snow and the winter. So much so, in fact, that I purposely avoid complaining about the heat in the summer so my friends will not label me as a whiner. I am not typically a complainer, but the facts are what they are. I live in the Northeast. For a few months out of the year, there will be snow and ice, and there's absolutely nothing I can do about it.

We can learn a lot from Mother Nature on how to approach life, health and money. First, we learn to control the things we can, and accept and deal with the things we cannot control. I'm not sure who came up with that philosophy, but I certainly agree with it. We know there will be snow in the winter just like we know there will be ups and downs in the stock market. We do not moan about it, do we? We plan for it and live with it. We know we are going to die, but if it is preceded by an unexpected illness, it makes little sense to ask God, "Why me?" It is just an eventuality we could not control.

There is no reason to expect to live a scripted life that conforms to an exact plan. We expect the unexpected. If you don't like the weather in New England, for example, just wait 10 minutes. If you think the Red Sox are going to win the World Series every year, then you must not be a student of history. Nobody made any promises to us when we were born about how life was supposed to be. Our birth certificates did not come with expiration dates on them, giving us the day of our death. Although, I have to say that, as creepy as that might be, it would make estate and financial planning a heck of a lot easier. No one ever told us we were entitled to have more money in retirement than we had during our working years.

I recently spoke with a 62-year-old man who insisted he was only going to live to be 75 years old. He made this assertion in spite of the fact that he had no apparent health issues. His rationale for this was that his parents only lived to their early 70s. He figured that was how it was going to be for him too. Fortunately for my client, that is not how life works. Statistics say he has an excellent chance of living longer than his parents did.

Nursing home planning also creates a similar reaction in some. Quite often, an unexpected health issue and an expensive nursing home stay can be the difference between wealth and bankruptcy. Still, some think it could never happen to them and they fail to plan. The next time you visit a nursing home or an assisted living facility, ask any of the residents you see waiting in the lobby for their loved ones a question. Ask them whether their stay here was an item they listed when drawing up their financial plan. Of course they did not. No one would! You hope it will not happen. But the fact that it does happen, and it happens often, will cause a prudent individual to plan for such a development just in case.

In order to have true financial, legal and mental health, we need to go through the check list of items we can control and conversely what we cannot control.

Health: A good start to maintaining excellent health would be to eat right, not smoke and exercise regularly. The flip side of living longer is that you could outlive your income, which is one of the most common fears among those approaching or in retirement, according to a January 2010 study put out by the Investment Company Institute. Other studies list running out of money in old age as being higher on the fear chart than death. Fear seems to have a paralyzing effect on many because many do not plan for this eventuality. Others hoard their money and lead a miserable life as a result. So what is the solution? Speak with a financial professional about a guaranteed income for life planning strategy. Understand what "risk free" investing is and take advantage of it. Try to get the biggest return you can without loss and you will be in good shape.

Legal Matters: No one can predict just when he or she will die. Nor can we predict how our family will react to issues surrounding our death. But what we can do is plan properly by preparing wills, trusts and other documents that make an unbearable situation more manageable for those we leave behind. You can leave your assets to your neighbor's dog if the paperwork is drawn up properly by a competent attorney. But good luck just doing nothing and hoping the owner of the dog can explain what your intentions were to the judge during the probate process. Proper legal planning means setting your situation up so that no matter what crazy curve ball life tosses your way, you will be ready. People assume that because you are making legal arrangements with wills and trusts, you are carving the future in stone and there can be no deviation. That is a myth, and it could get you in trouble.

Financial: Financial preparations should be based on age, income, desired lifestyle and risk tolerance. An effective financial plan will not remain static throughout your life. It will be tweaked and adjusted to accommodate whatever stage of life you attain. The closer you are to retirement, the more conservative your approach will be when it comes to investing. You don't want to be in a position where any of your savings could lost as you near retirement age. It is simply too hard to recover at that stage of the game. Before you risk your nest egg, ask yourself how much you can afford to lose without it affecting the quality of your life. The rich can take huge hits and not even blink. However, most of my clients and most people I know would have a significant lifestyle adjustment if half of their assets were to vaporize overnight due to some market event or some natural disaster on the other side of the globe.

As the Boy Scouts have said for more than 100 years, "Be Prepared." The motto is a simple one, and it appears to be stating the obvious, but you would be amazed at how many people do not heed such straightforward advice when it comes to their financial futures. Control what you can, accept what you can't and be prepared by planning for all of it.

CHAPTER SEVENTEEN

Clearing the Air About Annuities

"A lie gets halfway around the world before the truth has a chance to get its pants on."

-Sir Winston Churchill

I am not the type to buy into all of the crazy data and research that can sometimes overwhelm a person to the point of information overload. There are only so many facts and figures that can be presented and cause me to change my behavior and adjust my overall philosophy. However, for the last decade, I have worked in an industry where information is sometimes twisted and manipulated to persuade a person to buy into a concept that might not be in their best interests. For example, an annuity, which is just a word, has been the victim of a calculated smear campaign that rivals the dirtiest of mud-slinging in politics. The perpetrators of such nonsense tend to be institutions and individuals who benefit from you, as an investor, going in an alternative direction. They make money when you do what they say. Since their income is based on your keeping your money parked with them, it makes perfect sense for them to attack annuities because the basic premise of an annuity is that it makes payments back to you. That flies in the face of their business model, doesn't it? Doing a bit of math here, 1.5% of $1,000,000 is $15,000. That's what a firm will bring in per year as long as you keep your money with them. There is nothing wrong with their business model as a general rule. Good financial people deserve to be paid for their work. My issue is more with "bad" financial people who base their advice on their own interests and their own incomes instead of wrapping their business model around your needs and your income.

I host a radio show on one of the top talk radio stations in the Boston area. We spend a tremendous amount of time and effort assembling a lineup of topics and guests that represent all sides of the financial marketplace. Why? Because we want our listeners to have many opinions and ideas thrown their way so they can make informed and educated decisions for the betterment of their families' future. However, just before our program airs, there is another show on which the hosts universally, blindly, and carelessly bash annuity products, almost on a weekly basis. I'm sure you have similar offenders in your area, but these attacks are so egregious that there must be a reason, right? You bet. One of the show's hosts has created a cute nickname for herself, "Master of Mutual Funds" or something like that. She often begins and ends her annuity bashing with the idea that the only reason someone would "sell" you an annuity is because the "salesperson" makes 8% day one!

"They are getting rich off of you," she claims. Yet, as legendary radio host Paul Harvey always noted, "…and now, the rest of the story!"

What the host of this other show says is that because the salesperson is "making 8% on your money," the product being sold is not the right investment. She must be implying the proper investment can only be obtained by paying more! Let's table the 8% figure for the time being because anyone who knows the annuity industry knows that commissions vary, but rarely, especially in this day and age, are they that high. Let's say she charges her clients 1% (which is low) per year to manage their money. An annuity contract will vary in contract length from short terms, such as three years, to very long-term contracts of 20 years. But for the sake of this explanation, let's use the average annuity contract length that most annuity buyers use – 10 years.

Client one has $100,000 in an annuity. Over the 10-year span, the commission according to "Our Lady of Mutual Funds," or maybe it's

"Sweet Lady of Mutual Funds" (I promise to find out what the name is) would be $8,000. Client 2 has $100,000 with her firm. Again, assuming the low ball figure of 1%, that will result in a charge of $10,000 to the client. If your financial advisor doesn't know that $10,000 is more than $8,000, then you might want to find another person to handle your money. It's like a doctor asking you to drop your pants so they can take a look in your ears! If you don't know where the ears are located, find another profession.

The greater point is that making financial decisions is not about what the advisor makes. It's about what they do. I have no problem with a trained, honest professional making a lot of money. You shouldn't either! If they are delivering on what you need and you are making money, then the compensation is irrelevant.

What Is an Annuity?

The word "annuity" means nothing on its face, but the financial definition is – a product offered by an insurance company in which the funds within the account are protected to some degree and will earn an interest rate based on some type of predetermined crediting method. Annuities have other attributes, namely the payout options that will vary widely from product to product, and the additional protection features that also vary but can protect a policy holder from issues resulting from death, lawsuits and nursing home stays.

Again, On Money Matters television and radio, we spend an enormous amount of time making sure we expose our listeners/viewers to ALL areas of financial, legal and health concepts. Our focus is broad, not narrow. That way they can be as educated as possible and make the best decisions. Every financial product, from mutual funds, stocks and treasuries to annuities, bank CDs, REITS and insurance, has its place and function. Each should be viewed as a tool that could potentially help individuals reach their retirement goals. We would never throw a blanket over one particular area of finance just because we do not directly make money on those products or services. The last 10 years have shown that no stone should be left unturned. When a financial advisor downgrades a product such as an annuity, which has provided protection for millions of Americans in a time when people are sick of losing money in a volatile market, is not only bad advice but borders on the criminally slanderous. The "Mogul of Mutual Funds" if asked by a client for a financial vehicle that protects you from the downside of the market but offers upside growth with benefits for building income plans, would be silly saying "I know you want that, but since I don't make as much when you do that, let's try and confuse you so much about financial tools outside of what I do that your eyes glaze over, and we get back into the hypnotic state that made me a millionaire to begin with." Doesn't that sound like some Liam Neeson hostage movie?! Scary.

Client says, I want no risk, access to my money, some guaranteed growth and the overall feeling that everything will be OK.

"Mega Mamma of Mutual Funds" says, "Ok, I hear you, but let's do this – high-risk, access to your money only if the market is up…but if it is down and you withdraw money, you will be pulling a greater percentage of the overall account out, which will increase your chances of running out of money sooner. Oh, and did I mention that it will cost you more?"

I don't think I can say this enough: annuities, CDs, mutual funds, toilet seats or tire irons, are all are just tools. Tools mean nothing unless they are applied and given a purpose. Financial tools mean nothing until they are applied properly into a well thought out, careful financial strategy. Always consult a financial professional and be sure to express what you want rather than do what they want.

A hammer can be used to a build beautiful home, but it can also be used to break windows and thumbs. The tool itself is only as good as the hands that work its magic. A few unscrupulous advisors have used annuities, mutual funds, stocks, mortgages – and whatever else they can find – to take advantage of their unsuspecting victims. Look no further than Bernie Madoff and the billions of dollars he stole from vulnerable, trusting folks without, by the way, using annuities. Doctors, lawyers, teachers and used car salespeople – all can mislead and defame their industry, but it does not make the tools they use the enemy. Should chalkboards be banned if a teacher fails to teach a kid to read? Should BMWs be taken off the road if a salesperson convinces a customer to buy one when he or she cannot afford its payments? Should all stocks be labeled as bad investments when someone loses everything in the stock market?

Checking the Facts

Why defend annuities so vigorously? Well, according to multiple studies conducted and reports produced by such reputable sources as DSS Research, Larson Research and Strategy Inc. and the United States Government Accountability Office (GAO), our nation is prepping for an epidemic of massive proportions that deals directly with Baby Boomers running out of money sooner than expected. Many factors, including life expectancy, low savings rates, Social Security uncertainty, inflation, taxes and market volatility, contribute to this worry. But the overall concern is that financial planners are not making enough of an effort to put the focus back on income strategies. According to a recent GAO report commissioned by the Chairman of the Special Senate Committee on Aging, Sen. Herb Kohl from Wisconsin, Americans can avoid the risk of outliving their savings if they take some preventative steps now.

For one, understand how to maximize Social Security and use it to its fullest potential. Education is key, but not enough people in the financial world can even begin to educate their clients when they, themselves, remain uneducated in this area. The GAO also found that systematically drawing down your savings and converting a portion of the funds into an income annuity can be an effective way to build a foundation of guaranteed safe income in retirement. The GAO also concluded that an immediate annuity can protect retirees from the risk of outliving their savings but that only 6% of those with existing 401(k)'s actually purchased one at retirement.

A Fit for Some but Not for All

The uses of Fixed Indexed Annuities have demonstrated favorable results for individuals who are transitioning from their working years into retirement. This method allows them to protect their nest egg and get competitive returns with the option of converting into an income stream later in the contract. I like to use the example of New England Patriots Coach Bill Belichick running the ball in the fourth quarter, when the lead is enough to ensure a victory. It would be very uncharacteristic of him to have his quarterback throw the ball unnecessarily, or take chances when the game is under control and winning is the most important thing. Many, when they get to retirement age, will have just enough for them to get by as long as they don't make any stupid mistakes. Run the ball. Hold onto it for dear life. That is what an annuity can do for us financially.

So the question remains as to whether an annuity is right for you? This can only be answered by your imagining the situation where half of your assets vanish from a sudden market downturn, or some unforeseen life event. Could your lifestyle handle such a blow? If the answer is no, then you might be a suitable candidate for the type of secure income financial planning annuities provide.

Another segment of the population the GAO report points to as needing such planning are those individuals who lack traditional pensions that were, up until a few years ago, so commonplace in the American workplace. I suggest that people without the luxury of these now antiquated employer-sponsored pension plans begin thinking strongly about developing a private plan to fill that void. Income is never a fad that will be replaced by some flavor of the month concept. It will always be a need. Bills and expenses will never escape us.

The second study I found to be quite eye-popping was the "Reclaiming the Future" study by Allianz that surveyed 3,257 US adults between the ages of 44 and 77. The 2010 study revealed the following:

- Americans fear outliving their money more than they fear death itself.
- The economic downturn was a big "wake-up call" and annuity-like solutions are gaining significant relevance and appeal.
- Of the people surveyed who currently own annuities, 76% of them are happy with them.
- The reasons for their satisfaction had to do with protection from market downturns and an option for a guaranteed income for life.
- Annuities ranked second highest among consumers in customer satisfaction beating out mutual funds at 38%, stocks at 36%, U.S. savings bonds at 35% and CDs at 25%.

One oddity remains. When people are asked if they have a positive or negative feeling about annuities in general, many will still answer negative. What's puzzling, however, is the fact that when they are asked to describe their perfect investment, they inevitably describe the characteristics, benefits and features of – you guessed it – an annuity

A key finding of the study revealed that an overwhelming 80% of respondents preferred a product with a 4% return and a guarantee against losing value over a product with an 8% return that was vulnerable to market downturns. What this tells me, both as a consumer and financial professional, is the sentiment and overwhelming feeling of the general public is not understood by our industry, and we have truly failed to address it.

It is my contention that financial professionals should reevaluate their methods of educating their clients. I don't expect the entire financial community to embrace all financial tools and concepts with equal enthusiasm. That will never happen. But I do expect the community of financial professionals, of which I am a proud member, to recognize the needs and concerns of the people it claims to serve, and refrain from using false data and scare tactics to confuse the consumer. Yes, it is hard these days to know for sure whether or not the information we are getting is accurate and honest. That situation may never be thoroughly corrected. But if enough people in the financial world commit to open discussion and honest dialogue, the consumer will be the ultimate winner.

Ben Bernanke, Chairman of the Federal Reserve, is an owner of annuities. Basketball legend and Hall of Famer Shaquille O'Neal said the number one word in financial planning is "annuities." My mom, the person whom I care for the most when it comes to protection of income and assets, owns annuities. Those are three people who clearly benefited from the proper use of these products. Good thing there are financial people out there still willing to take less in terms of pay to offer you more.

Some of the features that make annuities popular savings tools for people in the modern era are the little "extras" that insurance companies are incorporating into the policies that make them more user-friendly.

The old way of looking at money had your income coming from three distinct and different sources. Number one was your company pension. It wasn't that long ago that the first pension was offered here in the United States by the American Express company in 1875. Shortly thereafter, the B&O Railroad, made famous by the board game Monopoly, offered them.

Fast forward to the 1980s and you will learn that over 51 million workers in the United States have a pension of some sort. A surge of employer-sponsored pension plans occurred when unions began bargaining for pension benefits in the early 1900s. Once life expectancy rates started to increase, especially after World War II, it became almost a certainty that you would have a pension at your current job. The first private pension account, or annuity contract, was set up through Met Life Insurance Company back in 1921. I don't mean to bore you with such detail, other than to stress that retirement income planning is nothing new.

Another source of retirement income that Americans could once rely on was the Social Security program. The idea was based on a long-held global tradition of governments taking care of their citizens. The ancient Greeks and the feudal lords of medieval Europe seemed to adopt a maternal sense for their people. However, no one would have ever thought the world would experience such mammoth growing pains in the period from the Industrial Revolution through World War II. Who could have foreseen the enormous growth and progress in the field of science and medicine, which resulted in a dramatic rise in life expectancy? All of this led to a situation where the solution no longer fit the problem.

Finally, our own individual savings or "nest eggs," as we so cutely refer to our cash reserves, were intended to pick up the slack, or fill in the gaps, where the first two options left off.

All we really have to go by when we do our future-gazing is the history that laid the bricks on which we walk today. However, things are sharply different in the post-recession, new millenium, instant message, Facebook age that we find ourselves in.

As more and more companies drop pensions from their list of employee benefits, it is becoming abundantly clear Social Security is incapable of keeping up with the cost of living. The full weight of responsibility falls on us, then, to make up the shortfall from our own personal savings. This burden is made worse by those in the financial profession who play fast and loose with these resources, putting them at risk at a time when the retiree needs them the most. So what do we do? Fortunately the modern annuity has emerged to fill the gaps. Since the insurance industry has taken the leading role in being the custodian of the annuity concept, you can automatically assume that protection features are going to be a huge part of why it works.

Let's think about what we need to protect ourselves in this modern financial age. Market crashes and stock market hits can not only be scary headlines, but they can be painful setbacks to people who wouldn't consider themselves billionaires. So many people lost most of their life savings back in 2008 that it was commonplace to see retirees and senior citizens back in line at the employment office. Ask yourself how your lifestyle would be affected if you woke up one day to discover over 60% of your assets had vanished?

Besides the obvious protection that an income stream from an annuity can provide, protection against stock market loss is the greatest benefit afforded by annuities. Originally, the annuity world offered a product that worked similar to the way a CD works. You selected a period of time to set your money aside, you were credited an interest rate that was typically fixed, and when the contract was complete you were free of any relationship. The advantage to having an annuity over a CD was usually the better interest rate and the flexible withdrawal options provided. The CD was usually a better option when the money deposited was earmarked for short-term obligations or emergencies.

Then the insurance industry , through focus groups, surveys and studies, began listening to what the public wanted in terms of a more advanced and modern solution. How can we offer an interest rate that is higher when the market climbs but protects the principle balance when the market dips? The Equity Index Annuity was born. More commonly referred to now as the Fixed Indexed Annuity, or FIA, this concept allows for greater participation when the stock market or economy swells, but promises a worst case zero interest return in a down or negative year. This feature was critical for the millions of annuity customers who could have lost nearly everything in 2008, yet were safe. Then in 2009, when the market corrected, FIA owners experienced some but not all of the gains. The insurance company "caps" your growth and removes the downside. This is a perfect fit for the investor who has enough to receive sufficient income, yet wants to run the clock out safely without taking needless risks.

CHAPTER EIGHTEEN
To Win at Planning, You Have To Vanquish Human Nature

"Courage is resistance to fear, mastery of fear, not absence of fear."
-Mark Twain

I'm not a big fan of most of the music I hear on the radio these days. Although I can tap my toe to a Lady Gaga song on occasion, her offstage acts wear me out. Mainstream television shows annoy me more and more as the years go by. I do not consider myself old-fashioned, but these reality shows just fail to entertain me. Frankly, I don't want to be offered a glimpse into the life of 15-year-old pregnant girls who are in cupcake battles while they are losing weight. I'm not a big fan of senseless reality competitions. I don't actually care who is getting voted off the island this week nor does it intrigue me to learn which star will out-dance another.

    I am constantly amazed at the capricious nature of the human psyche. People can be generous, kind, benevolent and understanding. They can also be miserly, self-centered, stingy and obtuse. When it comes to money and how we handle it, I have found there are many who, in the words of my high school English teacher, "have their minds made up and don't want to be confused by the facts."

Here we are, with the memories of 2008 freshly visible in our rear view mirror, and there are those who are still reluctant to correct major holes in their financial, legal and health situations. Some of this reluctance can be traced to their having put credence in rumors, preconceived notions and mistruths. As a financial professional, I fear that if this trend doesn't self-correct, we may be in for a financial epidemic that will rival the Great Depression of the 1930s.

Before you think me a doomsayer, consider something that came up while I was hosting my radio show, a program dedicated, naturally, to finance. We were discussing long-term care and how one could protect oneself from the devastating effects of a health crisis. I made mention of statistics from the United States Department of Health and Human Services about the likelihood of having something financially disastrous occur to you after you turn 65. Would you believe that the chances of that happening are over 60%? That is an eye-opening statistic, isn't it? The handwriting is on the wall, the prophets are preaching and the town criers are hoarse from saying it. People need to plan for this and do it now.

Preparing versus Procrastination

My work with people is largely one of solving problems. On my office wall are plaques, certificates and degrees that certify me as one who is qualified to give financial advice. But those are not as valuable to me, nor are they as much of a certification, as the personal credentials I have acquired through my own life experience. My family, and especially my mother, went through many years of difficulty, both financially and emotionally, after doctors diagnosed my grandmother with Alzheimer's disease. Those troubles impressed upon me how crucial it is to have a plan in place so one does not have to resort to 'managing by emergency.' There is nothing I regret more than having to sit across the conference table from a family in crisis and tell them there is nothing I can do to help them because it is too late. It was that way with one particular couple. At one time, they had the health and enough time and resources to safeguard themselves from the unforeseen occurrences that would eventually overtake them. But they procrastinated until it was too late. Then there are others I can remember who made appointments to discuss the possibilities of the future while there was still time to accommodate them.

It is my custom during initial interviews to sit and listen more than I talk. As I sat with the couple who had come into my office, I asked questions about their goals, dreams and aspirations and took notes on their responses. They were looking for a solution to a financial problem that was not necessarily unique to them. How could they take the money they had saved to this point, make it grow, protect it from financial evaporation and make it stretch throughout their retirement. They had several IRA accounts invested in stocks and mutual funds. These accounts had lost a large portion of their original value during two market crashes that had occurred in the past 11 years. They had attempted to "self-medicate" by moving their IRAs to extremely low-paying IRA CDs at banks that offered less than 2% rates of returns. This made the immediate pain go away. You might say it "stopped the bleeding."

Now at least their money was safe. But it wasn't a solution because their 2% return wouldn't even keep up with inflation. If they ever hoped to use their money to fund a comfortable retirement, something had to be done. Apparently, the financial professionals with whom they were dealing had never conveyed to them that safely losing ground is still losing ground. With inflation chipping away at the value of the dollar and with a renewal rate of less than 1%, their money was shrinking way too fast. They began to realize that what they had saved for retirement would not be enough. Like most people, their biggest fear was that they would retire, get too old to work and then run out of money. Fortunately for these folks, we were able to rescue their IRAs from the low-yielding bank CDs and place them into a product that paid out more interest, while at the same time ensuring them a guaranteed monthly income for life.

Feelings Are Facts and Fears Are Real

I remember being told as a small child that there was nothing to fear in the dark. "Close your eyes and go to sleep," my mother would say comfortingly. "There is nothing to fear in the dark."

She was right, of course, but I remained afraid of those imaginary terrors nonetheless – fears that only a four-year-old can have. My feelings, however unfounded, were facts. It is only natural that people treasure their independence. We like to have control of our lives as long as we possibly can. The fear of growing too old to work and then running out of money, is a legitimate concern. It happens to many retirees, unfortunately. If you were to take a poll asking individuals where they would want to spend time recovering from an accident or an illness – in an institution, like a hospital, assisted living facility, nursing home or in their own comfortable homes – the answer would overwhelmingly be the home. The fact of the matter is, however, that this is not a luxury Medicaid affords. Healing at home requires personal insurance to cover the cost, or personal savings.

The man and woman I was interviewing were relatively young – in their early 60s – and there was no reason why they couldn't expect to live a healthy, long, active life in retirement. But hearing the statistics revealed on the radio show made them start thinking about what could happen. Maybe they would be in the 40% who would never need long-term health care. But maybe they would land in the 60% who would. It was something they wanted to plan for if they could. What would happen to their money, their dignity, their freedom to make choices if they ever went into a nursing home, assisted living facility or rehab center?

In such situations, the obvious direction in which to look is toward a combination of estate planning steps that include protecting the value of their savings and working with an attorney to develop a plan to deal with the legal aspects of aging. In part, the solution called for using annuities, more specifically fixed indexed annuities, or FIAs. This "medicine" solved the broken money piece of the puzzle. The product gave them a rate of return that was linked to a specific index, such as the S&P 500 or the Dow Jones, but with no possibility of loss if the market should have another of its horrible episodes. They understood how the concept would work for them. They were willing to have some of the growth, or upside potential, trimmed away in return for the assurance that they could never go backwards again.

When the market lost more than half its value in the crash of 2008 and then recovered most of it in 2009, most people were struggling to get their heads back above water. During the same time, an owner of an FIA, such as the one this couple was considering, would be sitting pretty, having lost nothing in the downturn but enjoying the plusses of the recovery from an uninjured position. This accounts for why FIA owners at cocktail parties after a market crash weren't in a state of panic.

The FIA also has some built-in features that promise certain guaranteed rates of growth for money to be used as income down the road. The plan this couple was considering promised a rate of 8.2%. Their money sits in an account built by the IRS with real defined rules and regulations on how the money is to be spent. With these rules already in place, it is natural that anything that can be taken advantage of for the purposes of income should be immediately snatched up.

The next feature this account would provide to this couple was a built-in home care/long-term care benefit that could trigger additional money if the time came in which their health failed. Features such as this have been included in many FIAs over the past eight years, mainly due to the public's fear of being unprepared for long-term care and the expense that goes with it.

What about Liquidity?

One legitimate downside to using these types of accounts is that during the first 10 years or so, you can only access up to 10% of your account per year without paying some type of charge. But otherwise, there are no downsides I can see. The accounts cost nothing in the way of fees.

In the case of this couple, the funny thing was that they were paying a fee anyway with their current IRA, without the benefit of taking anything out. Also, because the money had been set aside for retirement income, 100% total liquidity was not seen by them as so important that they should exchange total liquidity for the paltry growth rate of a CD.

If you were to put $50,000 into a saving account, allow it to earn virtually nothing, would you really sleep well? Investors know their money needs to be working for them at all times. Older investors also know their money needs to be working for them at all times, but they are more sensitive to risk. This couple expressed appreciation that their fears and concerns were finally being addressed. They said they felt relieved they had finally been able to sit down with a financial advisor who specialized in income planning for the modern retiree.

When they understood their retirement income could be guaranteed for life and their concerns about long-term care were addressed, I could almost see relief flood their countenances and the color return to their faces. Every nuance of this plan was music to their ears. Every color, taste and sound of this plan was pleasing – all but one. The name. Yep, you heard me right. Somewhere along the line, they had been prejudiced against annuities. But strip the name away, and they loved what it did for them. It's like someone asks for ice cream. They are served ice cream. They taste it. It tastes wonderful. They love the creamy texture. And the flavor is just right.

"Say, what kind of ice cream is this," they ask.

"Vanilla."

"Vanilla? Why, I hate vanilla! Could you give it to me again and just call it something else? I hate vanilla."

I know, it sounds a bit crazy, doesn't it? But that's how much sense it makes to like everything about a product except its name. Frankly, I think they should be called something else. The word "annuity," even though I know what it means and why they are called that, just doesn't fit anymore. Let's call them "safe payers," or "do-it-yourself pensions" or "retirement contracts." I think strawberries are misnamed too. Call them "redberries" because they have nothing to do with straw.

In a recent survey, a thousand conservative investors were asked to construct and describe their perfect financial product. Almost 98% of those surveyed described annuities as their ideal choice. Yet only 40% of those same people had a positive opinion of annuities. That says something pretty profound. Somewhere along the line, their thinking was influenced in the negative. It could have been by an angry radio talk show host. Or it could have been something said by a desperate financial advisor afraid of losing a client's business. Somewhere, they heard something bad about annuities. When you ask for specifics as to why this impression exists, most can't tell you.

The evidence is overwhelming that most of the bias felt against annuities is unfounded. The Wharton School of Business recently conducted an unbiased study on FIAs and how they have performed. The statistics reveal they have consistently outperformed most risk-weighted mutual funds. At this writing, articles are appearing in several financial journals and magazines that spell out how the current administration is actively promoting the use of annuities to ward off future income crises. I am even seeing, finally, well written, thoughtful pieces in all the major news outlets proclaiming that the mainstream financial world had it all wrong. Even with all of that going on, some people still can't get past a deeply rooted idea, regardless of how irrational that idea may be. Like I said. feelings are facts and, sometimes, no amount of evidence building or reasoning can change them.

This isn't being said to belittle the decision made by that couple. Personally, I admire people for trusting their instincts sometimes. I am reminded of that old automobile commercial that compared the old with the new, "This is not your father's Oldsmobile." Annuities used to have long surrender periods and did not have the income and long-term care features they do today. Then, the public cried out for answers and solutions, and the insurance industry stepped up to the plate and provided them. Professionally, I am happy to be able to solve problems with products that prevent market loss but still capture market gains. I am thrilled to be able to offer clients a contractual agreement that pays them a handsome return on their savings – one that will allow them to celebrate all their hard work during their golden years. And these modern planning methods aren't exclusive to just annuities. Today, there are several options available that weren't there a decade ago.

Expanding Our Horizons

My goal in working with television and radio shows, and with the print media projects I have underway, is to pull back the curtain and allow people to see all sides of a solution. It is too tough of a world out there not to try and entertain every possible avenue to potentially better yourself. In speaking engagements, I try to convey how vital it is to expand our horizons to see all there is when it comes to financial planning options. I have to confess, however, that it angers and frustrates me to see the greed of a few in the financial industry motivate them to purposely sow seeds of distrust for their own gain. I felt bad for this couple. They had so much more than so many others I see every day. But they allowed themselves to be prevented from taking proper steps in a direction that would have truly benefited them because of misinformation and unfounded rumors.

Not a Big Fan, But…

I am not a big fan of airplanes. But if I need to get from Boston to Los Angeles in one day, I will fly on one. I am not a fan of the dentist. I don't even like the sound of the word "dentist." But if I expect to keep all of my teeth when I am 70 years old, I will see the dentist regularly. And if I want to keep all of my hard-earned money, see it earn a competitive rate of return, guarantee me an income for life, fight inflation and serve as the cornerstone of a financial plan that can do all the above while still protecting me from the perils of a long-term care disaster, then I suppose I don't need to like annuities – but by God, I will use them.

CHAPTER NINETEEN

Some Things that Glitter Just May Be Gold

"Two roads diverged in a wood, and I... I took the one less traveled by, and that has made all the difference."

- Robert Frost

Perhaps you have heard one of these the old axioms:

- "There is no such thing as a free lunch."
- "If it sounds too good to be true, it probably is."
- "All that glitters isn't gold."

Don't get me wrong here. Being careful is what I do for work. But it seems to me sometimes that we have become an overly cautious society. I believe we have become so jaded in our view of the world that we sometimes miss out on legitimate opportunities. Caution is a good thing, mind you. I have owned an asset protection firm in the Plymouth, Mass., area for more than a decade now, and we make our living pointing out the safe route to financial success. But sometimes that which glitters is gold, and it is in our best interests to know the difference between glittery programs that are worthless and truly worthwhile strategies that could help create wealth for us. While our tough, non-penetrable exterior shield is a protection, it is in our best interests not to allow it to shield us from all the good things that are available to us. I am a big fan of another idiom when it comes to making financial decisions: "Don't throw the baby out with the bath water."

What is a "Pre-Owned Annuity?

There has been much discussion in the financial world recently about a relatively new financial opportunity involving structured settlement transfers, sometimes referred to as "pre-owned annuities." In recent months, we have made a concerted effort to educate the public, as well as certain clients, on the advantages of these strategies. One of the significant upsides to an account like this is the rate of return can be as high as 7% without market risk. Because of the legal assignment feature of these instruments, the rate can be guaranteed. Most of the time, when people are looking for a short-term parking place for a portion of their money, they will look to bank CDs. Interest rates for CDs may have been 5%- 6% a few years ago, but that is unrealistic nowadays. According to Bankrate.com, the national average interest on CDs at this writing is less than 1%.

When it comes to understanding structured settlement transfers, people sometimes fail to understand the actual reason why you get that factored rate on your cash. Here's why. When an A-rated insurance company sends you a check each month, or a lump sum at the end of the year, they are not the ones who are generating the generous return. You are actually purchasing future payments that already exist from another individual at a substantial discount. That is where the benefit is.

Keep in mind the entire transaction must take place in a court of law, thanks to a little obscure line in the IRS tax code, IRC 5891, which threatens a hefty excise tax penalty to an individual who embarks on this journey without going through the proper channels. Initially this might sound like a complicated transaction, but it really isn't. Anytime something new is introduced to the general public, the reaction among many is to want to know how every single moving part works. It is not necessarily an improper impulse. We did it when horseless carriages first rolled down

Main Street. The same spirit of curiosity captured the American public when the Wright Brothers made their brief, historic flight in Kitty Hawk, NC.. We are inquisitive. We want to know to know how things work, and we want answers right now. Still, you cannot imagine an investor walking into his or her neighborhood bank demanding to know how the CD they are investing in generates the rate it does. We rely on the bank and accept that it is what it is. As long as they produce the return on the back end that they promised on the front end, we are all smiles. It is the same with SSTs. Worry about the nuts and bolts of the product is better left to the professionals and the institutions involved. However, for those who are not content to know the time of day but insist on knowing how the watch works, any competent financial advisor should be able to answer your questions.

As far as investments go, it is comforting to know that when you put your money into an SST you will get a lot more back when you take it out. That is why people invest in the first place, isn't it?

For some reason, and one I can't fully understand, some people have had a difficult time letting go of the idea that CDs and money market accounts are still a viable place to invest. It is my observation that people of this mindset have certain personality traits in common. They are usually people of extreme caution. They insist on safety above all else. They also do not like change. They share a general distrust of the financial world. They are impressed by buildings with columns and brick facades.

"Too good to be true!" I hear that a lot. But what the expression sometimes means is, "Too involved for me to think about and gather the intelligence I need to understand it." Most people who make a living in the finance world know what they know and are comfortable working within that sphere. Rarely do they branch out to other concepts or strategies. This is evident by the one-sided war waged against insurance companies by Wall Street money managers who fuel their massive yachts with monthly fees and charges. To those professionals who aspire to a full, well-rounded approach in their practice, I apologize. I did not mean to lump you in with the armchair advisors who care more about their renewals than they do about changing their strategies to fit the current conditions that plague the middle-class investor.

"Get Busy Livin'"

Structured settlement transfers are not products that people should jump into blindly. But with the education that cutting edge financial advisors are disseminating regarding SSTs, these unique products are becoming thought of more and more as certainly a better place to put money than in bank CDs, which promise virtually no interest. Perhaps the same thought process that would allow an investor to hand over a large sum of money to a bank for little or no interest, could, with education, motivate them to see the value of an alternative investment – one that would allow them to travel and enjoy life to a greater degree. A famous philosopher once said that an unexamined life is not worth living. Put simply, he meant that we should contemplate our actions in depth. For lack of a better way of putting it, we need to exercise our brains. I remember a scene from the 1994 movie, The Shawshank Redemption, based on a short story by Stephen King set in a New England Prison. At one point in the movie, the innocent protagonist, Andy Dufresne (Tim Robbins), tells his jail cell neighbor, played by Morgan Freeman, "Either get busy livin' or get busy dyin'." Sitting still and doing nothing out of a misplaced sense of caution gets you nowhere. Thinking can be hard work, which explains why so few people engage in it.

Not too long ago, I sponsored a client appreciation dinner. This is where every client whom we have helped, either in estate planning, asset protection or developing a retirement strategy, is invited to a restaurant where our firm picks up the tab for a nice meal, after which we bring them up to date on what's going on in the financial world and answer questions. It's completely free. They are already clients and I have no interest in selling them anything or obligating them to anything. They are even encouraged to bring a friend to the event. So, yes, Virginia, there really IS a free lunch (or dinner) sometimes! And yes, some financial products and strategies out there are capable of yielding high rates of return while still maintaining their status as guaranteed, safe investments.

CHAPTER TWENTY

When You See Bias in the Media, Follow the Money Trail

"It takes tremendous discipline to control the influence, the power you have over other people's lives."

-Clint Eastwood

In my opinion, the two segments of commerce that do the most miserable job of representing themselves in the electronic media are the financial profession and the medical profession. I am not a doctor. Just entering the doors of a hospital makes me queasy and the sight of blood makes me faint.

Is it just me, or are we turning into a nation of hypochondriacs? The television and the internet seem to feed the hysteria. Have you ever heard this news tease – "Is your home making you sick? Tune in at eleven and find out how to get help." Ouch! That would make any homeowner crazy! Or, maybe you have heard the announcer say, "Does your child have a head cold? Why a runny nose might be a sign that you need to rush to the emergency room! Join us at eleven."

Try searching for information on the symptoms of your cold on some of the medical websites on the internet, and you are likely to learn that you just could have a brain tumor, or perhaps some rare form of cancer. There was a time when I literally thought I had anthrax poisoning from information I found on a popular medical website.

The financial world represents itself poorly sometimes, issuing blanket advice, broad assumptions, scare tactics and sales pitches. Every item presented seems to be operating on the premise that whatever they are discussing applies to everyone within earshot. Let's not forget that the media are typically either made up or supported by agenda-driven corporate entities that want to lead you by the nose for their own self-interests. If you are puzzled by the biased content of a radio or television show, or a magazine article, check out who is advertising.

There is nothing un-American about promoting oneself. I do it. I host a radio program and I write a weekly column. I take part in many online blogs that involve financial education. Am I promoting myself? Of course! Do I offer my opinions? You betcha! But what I hope to accomplish is to develop a forum in which people can get the information they need to make intelligent decisions. I want to communicate viable strategies that fit individual circumstances and do it in such a way that does not try to elevate one approach by unfairly pushing another one down.

For years, the mainstream financial world of brokers and Wall Streeters has been besmirching and maligning insurance products, such as annuities and life insurance. This is not because those products or strategies are not effective or relevant, but they do so for the sake of their own profits. It reminds me of the question I hear from many people about energy – "Why don't we see any alternative forms of energy yet?" The reason is that it would take cash from the oil companies and divert it somewhere else. Forget the overall benefit to the country. It's the same with alternative financial vehicles. I would say that most of the advice given by the talking heads on television or in the columns of magazines is tainted by the motives of the advertisers. It has been my observation that some financial professionals, when cornered by a competing product and faced with losing a client, are tempted to say or do just about anything to keep the competition away. That is why we are witness to so much confusion and doublespeak. It is the client who is hurt by the misinformation and bogus education. It is the greedy businessman who benefits.

Right after the economic meltdown of 2008, when many saw how unreliable the stock market could be, millions of Americans went running to the safety and guaranteed growth of annuities. Some of those who form the cadre of counselors in the traditional financial world were still saying, "Annuity…bad!" (Insert caveman grunt here.) Those millions of Americans who sought the safety of insurance products certainly benefitted from that decision. Many saw their portfolios actually thrive.

Let me set the record straight. By no means do I intend for this to be a soap box sermon on the value of annuities. I'm just using that as an example. The same point could be made about the vilification of reverse mortgages, life insurance, real estate or whatever may exist outside the traditional mutual fund investment. They, too, have been arbitrarily demonized by some in the media purely for profit motives.

The goal here is to direct you to some great resources you probably won't see on MSNBC or read about in the Wall Street Journal. Granted, both of those media outlets are useful and they are part of my daily routine. But the advertisers control the content to such an extent that the bias against alternative strategies to the acquisition, preservation and distribution of wealth has become an invisible wall of prejudice of which many are not aware.

CHAPTER TWENTY-ONE

Avoiding the Specter of Final Expense

"I'm not afraid of death; I just don't want to be there when it happens."

— Woody Allen

I'm a pretty fun guy by nature. It goes against my grain to dwell too long on subjects like the one I am about to cover next. I have a feeling I am not the only one who likes to avoid morbid subjects. So how about we do this? I will write about a very important topic but try to do so in a way that will be informal, sometimes funny without the "creepy factor" that is ever so prevalent when discussing funerals.

I am going to go out on a limb here and say that 98.9% of the people who are reading this book will, at some point in their lives, die. Whether we like it or not, that is a proven, scientific fact. In case it has escaped your notice, this is an event that comes with a price tag. Since you won't be here to stroke the check for this part of the business, it could fall to someone in your family to pay the bill. According to the most recent statistics that I could find, according to the National Funeral Directors Association, the average cost for a funeral in the United States is $6,560. Throw in a vault and that jumps to $7,755. Please keep in mind this is an average and it includes some areas of the country where they toss you in a cardboard box and toast you into the afterlife with a bottle of Mr. Daniels' best whisky. But it also includes funerals where they treat the "guest of honor" to a shower of goodbyes as he or she lies in repose in a gold-plated box made by the Lamborghini Automotive group.

"Paperwork Just In Case"

We all like to think we are bullet-proof and immortal, especially when we're young. I suppose it is human nature. But far too many of us fail to plan for what happens in the end. Either we are not willing to accept it, or we just wish to avoid the subject. I know some folks who refuse to purchase life insurance or draw up a will because they feel this very action will somehow attract the attention of the Grim Reaper and serve as a macabre invitation for him to come for them. Although a frank discussion and an honest look at end-of-life planning may be anathema to some, others look upon it as just being the right and responsible thing to do.

You would think that, no matter who you are, you would want to express your wishes for your exit when you, as Shakespeare put it, "shuffle off this mortal coil." Wouldn't it be better to make health-related choices now by creating a power of attorney, rather than foisting them off on relatives, if you should find yourself in a situation where you could not articulate your wishes? That would certainly take the guesswork out of things and make it easier on your loved ones. Would it not make sense to make plans for your funeral ahead of time instead of letting such decisions tear at the fabric of your family later? All it takes are a few paragraphs that express how you wish for your remains to be treated before, during and after the ceremony.

Whatever the case, you should sit down with an attorney as soon as possible to get the basic estate planning documents done. These documents include a will, a power of attorney, health care proxy and perhaps other documents the attorney may suggest depending on your unique circumstances. Any competent financial advisor should be able to point you in the right direction. If you are squeamish, simply view this as "paperwork just in case." Just like you would not go to a podiatrist for a heart problem, make sure you find the right attorney. That can be difficult if you are left with a phone and the Yellow Pages. Most financial professionals have links to people on the legal side of things. Financial planning and estate planning usually intersect with legal planning. Please keep in mind that this type of planning can be done at any age.

Procrastination Is Easy

I know what it's like to struggle with procrastination in this regard. When my wife and I were buying our first home, we said, "After we buy the house, we will get the will done." Then after the birth of our first child, we repeated the pledge. We procrastinated, however, arguing to ourselves that it would be pointless if we had to change it if another child came along, or we bought another home. But at some point, we wised up and came to realize that life continues and, looking at it that way, we would continue putting it off indefinitely.

As we get a bit older and start to recognize a few more of the names printed in the obituary section of the newspaper, the reality of what will eventually happen to us becomes easier to see. That's when most people begin considering planning for that phase of life. Pre-planning a funeral includes both planning for the details of the event itself, but also for how it will be paid for. Most of my clients have shown me accounts where they set aside funds for that purpose. They were doing the right thing, of course – trying to make sure they were not leaving a financial burden for anyone else when they died. But usually, if not done with the aid of a professional, even the most careful planning may contain holes.

Filling In the Holes

Hole number one could be what type of account it is. What about access to the account? What most people fail to remember is the existence of the probate process in which an individual's assets are essentially frozen for a period of time following a death to allow for a legal settlement of the estate to take place. A certificate of deposit left in the bank, even though it may be set aside for the funeral expenses, might not accessible by your heirs for a least a year after your death. This means your loved ones will have to come up with the money themselves. That could present a struggle for some of them, putting family members in a tough financial spot. To avoid this, folks might want to consider an account with a beneficiary attached. This allows you to name whomever you wish as the designated recipient of the funds at your death. This will ensure the one you select will be able to access the funds right away. Because such a contract contains a designated beneficiary, it will avoid probate and perhaps taxes as well. This puts no one in a difficult financial situation that will create any negative lasting impressions. I plan on leaving this dimension with a clean track record and having everyone remember me fondly.

Hole number two is protecting the funds you earmark for final expense from evaporation due to the high cost of illness or nursing home expenses. You do not want them to be vulnerable. So often, we hear of people losing everything to the cost of illness or nursing homes. This is a subject that deserves an entire book, and at some point, I will attend to it. But for now, it is vital to know the steps to take to ensure that if you do leave money behind, it won't be susceptible to asset recovery due to a medical situation. Many financial advisors are now advocating funeral trusts for this reason.

These trusts are designed to be a safe place to deposit funeral earmarked funds and allow them to be totally shielded from the chaos resulting from a Medicaid situation. During the Medicaid process, families are sometimes put through the financial wringer, as they attempt to access every last penny that exists in various accounts. Usually, Medicaid will instruct the person to account for every last dime from accounts the government does not deem "Medicaid friendly." A Funeral Trust is fundamentally life insurance. Life insurance is considered to be an excellent place for funeral funds, but it can also be considered a cash asset by the powers that be. A good rule of thumb is that if there is any cash value associated with your life insurance, you should speak with a professional on how best to position that money as it pertains to estate planning. A funeral trust is a simple and effective tool for that.

Pre-Purchasing Funerals

If you are the hands-on type who really wants to get in there and tackle the specifics, then pre-purchasing a funeral might be the way to go for you.

Go to the funeral home of your choice and ask to speak with the director. From there, you can purchase the casket, organize the event itself, pick the songs and readings and pay for it right then. The advantage is obvious. The disadvantage is that people don't like the idea of having to do it. Although most of this can be done without stepping into a funeral home, it is sometimes the easiest way to ensure your wishes will be accommodated. If it is deemed by the powers above that you have a controlling personality, well, that will dealt with well into the afterlife.0

One thing to keep in mind is that the price of today's funeral might be different from one you are given on your big day. Since we have no way of predicting when we will die, we can't say just what things will cost down the road. The price of gasoline to transport your body will change. The flowers adorning your casket may cost more. They could even cost less, but that is not likely. Newspapers now charge for expanded obituaries and who knows what the rates will be then. Church services may require compensation. The items are endless. With so many uncertainties regarding our final "bill," it's worth speaking to the right professional about it now instead of letting the specter of our exit costs haunt our living years.

CHAPTER TWENTY-TWO

Preparing for Turbulent Times Ahead

"The time to repair the roof is when the sun is shining."
— John F. Kennedy

From an economic standpoint, there are dark clouds on our horizon, and I would like to use this chapter to point them out and suggest necessary steps readers may take to protect themselves. While I sometimes use amusing anecdotes to get my points across in the media, in this instance I need to be serious, because I believe the situation is serious.

In America, turbulent times lie ahead for our economy. Just who it will be that gets sucked into the spiraling vortex will come down to who is prepared for it and who is not. If history is any indication, the last economic free fall left many people frozen in fear and unable to make any accommodations, let alone form coherent thoughts. Hopefully, the next downturn will attack a more prepared nation.

Warning Signs

At the time this book was published, we were on the edge of our seats waiting to see if the US government was going to steer the ship clear of the impending fiscal cliff we were headed toward on Jan. 1, 2013. This is when the Bush era tax cuts were set to expire and send the nation into a tax spiral. The fear is that not only will experiencing a tax increase by default cost the average American thousands of dollars in additional taxes, nearly every economist and financial expert I am aware of expects that such an event will trigger a deeper recession than the one that occurred in 2008. If losing 60% in 2008 wasn't enough for you to do something about your financial plan, then don't worry, this next one will clean out the rest of your savings and it will become a moot point.

What are some of the warning signs? Well, besides the aforementioned "cliff," at this writing we have miserable job numbers, depressing real estate data and public confidence in the economy is at an all-time low and dropping. Fuel prices continue to escalate. When the price of a gallon of gasoline goes up, it affects far more than just our summer vacation plans. The issue goes much deeper than what campground to visit and how far it is from your home. Higher fuel prices represent an extra $100 billion coming out of the pockets of an already tapped out consumer. As I am writing this, the recession that began in 2008 is reported to have ended in 2010 and the economy is said to be in recovery. Is it real? Or, is the economic recovery we think is happening really just smoke and mirrors, artificially manufactured by Washington for the benefit of the next election? When it costs you and me upwards of $80 to fill up a 20-gallon tank, just the action of getting to work becomes one of the biggest reasons we need to get there. Getting to work is, of course, not a problem for the millions who are, as of this writing, unemployed.

Insiders have speculated to me that it will not be out of the realm of possibility to see gasoline prices touch $5 per gallon in the near future. According to a 2012 AAA report, per-gallon gasoline prices in other countries make pump prices in the United States look like a bargain by comparison. If you live in Turkey, for example, you pay around $10 per gallon. In England, the price is around $8 per gallon, and in India, it will cost you slightly over $5 per gallon. Is the U.S. behind the curve? Will the price we pay for gasoline soon equal or exceed that of the rest of the world? Should we get used to forking out even more for the privilege of driving our cars when our fragile economy is already on the brink?

There is a direct link between higher fuel prices and the higher costs we pay for other goods and services, such as food, shipping, air fares and appliances.

There is talk of alternative energy, and we do have hybrid vehicles, but what will it take before we get deadly serious about getting rid of fossil fuels entirely? Will oil prices have to hit $10 per gallon? Should we reconsider offshore drilling after what happened in the Gulf of Mexico?

The Debt Time Bomb

The next clue that we may be in for even harder times came in the recent news that the United States debt outlook, as measured by the S&P, has gone from "stable" to "negative," according an April 18, 2011, article in the Wall Street Journal. The AAA sovereign credit rating the U.S. currently enjoys at the time of this writing is endangered by a negative debt outlook. Some economic experts warn the rating is in serious danger of being lowered. What difference does this make? It means that US businesses will have difficulty borrowing. This will retard the country's economic growth even more. Without growth, we cannot solve the unemployment issue. Without people working, we cannot fix the mortgage crisis and stimulate home purchases.

To me, the solution seems simple and yet mostly ignored. Rather than make it more difficult for medium-sized and small businesses to operate by imposing unrealistic costs and levying even more suffocating taxes, why not encourage them to grow and hire by cutting taxes? That would be fixing problems from within, as opposed to the government's solution, which seems to be heaping more taxes and red tape on the backs of small business.

If I am having household budget issues and I am unable to balance my household books because there is more money going out that coming in, I cannot keep going to my employer to ask for more money. I need to curb my spending habits and learn to live within my means.

I could go on and on about how the government needs to step aside and allow industry and the economy to flourish on its own without interference, but the intent of this chapter is to warn readers to prepare for what I believe appears inevitable. Are you ready for what the next few years may yield in the way of economic difficulty? Ask yourself if you are prepared to lose 30% or more of your assets in another market downturn? Will you still be able to enjoy your current lifestyle if that were to happen? If the answer is no, then you need to take action now. There are plenty of strategies and concepts that are specifically tailored for people in that great cluster of middle- and upper-middle-income folks who simply cannot take another blow to their savings.

Income planning trends are forcing people to look at the next 10-15 years as pension rebuilding periods that are strategically set up to get the highest monthly amount possible and have that income guaranteed for life. I am finding that 99% of the people who walk through my office door are more concerned with running out of money in the future than they are about their health or even dying early. That is why I recommend that you sit down with your financial professional and ask how you can develop a plan that fits with your philosophy and your life goals. If your financial goals focus more on growth and less on preservation and distribution, then find a planner who can offer advice on the same. If, however, your goals focus more on securing a guaranteed income you cannot ever outlive, then you will need to find an advisor who can speak that language.

Think of it like seeking medical advice or treatment. How many adults still go to see their pediatrician? Once you reach adulthood, you stop going to your pediatrician, not because the doctor has lost competency but because you have grown up and require an expert whose focus is on adult medical care. The older you become, you will experience even more physical changes, which may require yet another doctor, with yet another area of expertise.

It's the same with financial planning. Your plan when you are 20 years old should be totally different when you reach 50. Adapting to what's ahead for you physically, as well as financially, is vital to remaining healthy in both areas. "Set it and forget it" does not work well when your situation is subject to change and yet that is how many people still do it when it comes to financial and estate planning.

I advise anyone who reads this to have a plan that allows them to adjust their risk. The world is filled to the brim with risk. There are many things we cannot control. If you take nothing else from this chapter, please take this one thought: Control the things you can control, accept the things you cannot and be as prepared as possible for hazards. The yellow caution light is blinking.

CHAPTER TWENTY-THREE

Braving a Snowstorm to Solve An Estate Problem

"Death ends a life, not a relationship."
— Mitch Albom, Tuesdays with Morrie

A few years ago, Keith Ellis, my business partner, and I battled driving snow and torturous winds to get to Nocera's Restaurant in Brockton, Mass., to speak to a group about retirement. The topic was "Twelve Roadblocks to Financial Success." Weather conditions worsened after we set out. One concern was getting there. The other was whether anyone else would come. We fully expected to walk into an empty room.

One thing I admire about New Englanders, however, is their toughness and their seeming willingness to brave virtually any storm. The room was packed. They had all thumbed their noses at something as silly as the year's fiercest nor'easter.

Typically, at a financial workshop such as this, the people come to learn about money matters in general and to enjoy good meal in a warm room in the company of people of their same age group. The event also serves as a non-threatening atmosphere and neutral environment in which Keith and I have the opportunity to answer questions and meet new potential clients. Once we distribute the handouts and make sure our audience is comfortably seated, we spend the next 50 minutes or so discussing such topics as income planning, Medicare, Social Security, probate issues and the power of trusts. Once done with that, we open it up to questions. This is my favorite part of the workshop. We try to circulate around the room, answering as many questions as possible.

Questions and Answers

Because our robust attendees had made such a heroic effort just to come to our workshop, we felt determined to give them as much of our experience and knowledge we possibly could. Outside, near hurricane force winds heaped snowdrifts and we knew there was no point in leaving early. As long as they had questions, we felt obliged to stay and provide answers. We wanted to make our journey count, and we felt as if it would have been disrespectful to those in attendance to let their journeys be wasted.

One couple struck me right from the beginning as people who didn't exactly fit into the stereotypical mold of those we usually encounter at these events. The husband looked to be in his mid to late 70s and his wife appeared to be quite a bit younger. She did not look quite like 20 years of age, but she did not look to be 60 either. Somewhere in between. I fought the inclination to pat the man on the back and congratulate him on landing such a pretty young lady. We would meet many fascinating people that night, but, as things would turn out, this couple prove to be exceptionally so. I did not know it at the time, but as events would unfold, they would lead me to a discussion I could little imagine and would not soon forget.

An Interesting Case Presents Itself

We made the one-hour trip back to Plymouth in just less than four hours. We knew the next day would consist of shoveling the snow from our driveways and making sure that our kids had plenty to do during their snow holiday from school. The following day would also consist of something that Keith and I always did as a matter of courtesy, which was to call all of the previous night's attendees to make sure we answered all their questions and that their overall experience was a pleasant one. As the calls came and went, I arrived at the phone number of the couple whose ages were so obviously different.

From a standpoint of financial planning, I had enough experience to know that a couple with such a pronounced age difference may need specialized help in developing a workable strategy. Statistics confirm that men die before the women in their lives. Given the age difference between this man and woman, it was almost a certainty who would outlast whom. I chatted briefly with the husband, and then had a more prolonged conversation with the wife. She knew her husband well. He liked to do things on his own. He was not quick to ask for or receive suggestions or help from professionals, regardless of their field of expertise. As I talked with the woman, I could hear a younger voice in the background and offered to let them get back to their company. The wife informed me that their daughter was there, staying with them for the duration of the storm.

The conversation shifted to how the couple's young adult daughter lived on her own in public housing, dealing with disabilities that made it difficult for her to be as totally independent as she wished. One of her mother's fears was that, after her husband's death, she would be left alone to care for their daughter, both physically and, of an even more major concern, financially.

As far as handling their financial affairs, the couple had done everything right for the most part. They were frugal spenders and avid savers. They protected themselves by purchasing Long-Term Care Insurance. They paid off the mortgage of the home in which they lived. They put aside a significant amount of money for their young daughter so she would be set for life. One issue plagued them, however. That was how their disabled daughter would be able to handle the money in case something happened to both of them. How could they make sure no one would take advantage of her?

I asked the woman if they had done any legal planning in the past five years. When she answered no, I knew this was an appointment I had to set. These people needed help. I told them there was an enormous hole in their estate plan, and it was it was imperative they fill it if they wished to be able to sleep well at night in the future. This touched a nerve with them and appropriately so. They had adopted this beautiful young girl when she was a baby. Her biological mother had refused to stop taking drugs, even during her pregnancy, causing the girl to suffer developmental issues. Although the young woman overcame so much and was coping magnificently with her disabilities, it was obvious she would require some type of assistance from others for the rest of her life.

We set the appointment and I enlisted the assistance of an attorney I often partnered with in such cases. We explored all of their goals and concerns. In a little while, we felt we knew this family pretty well and were ready to make suggestions. First, we needed to produce a document for the couple that would express in legal terms exactly how their daughter would be cared for in the case of her parents' death. This would require the use of a special needs trust, a document that detailed the who, what, where, when and how of their daughter's care. The next step was to fund the trust so the money would be there when the time came.

Fortunately for the couple, they had set aside enough. They were thrilled to learn the growth of the fund could be enhanced and distribution guaranteed. Since the wife was in her 50s and in sound health, we were able to place approximately $150,000 into a single premium life insurance policy that would leave a guaranteed death benefit of $621,706 tax-free and probate-free for the daughter. That was music to their ears. The details of the plan would also allow the couple to use the cash value from the policy to spend as they wished while they were alive...if they wanted to, that is. But the main reason for the plan was to make certain their beautiful daughter would be cared for to the fullest extent possible in the event that both parents passed away.

A Twist of Fate

My lawyer friend drew up a revocable special needs trust that included all of the important details, such as power of attorney forms, health care proxy documents, and the ever-important will. When the couple expressed their gratitude for having this enormous weight lifted from their family, they mentioned wryly how ironic it was that they had a snowstorm to thank.

"We weren't supposed to even be there," the husband said with a laugh.

I asked him what he meant. He explained that it was his brother who received the invitation to the workshop but was reluctant to go because of the storm.

"I told my brother that, if it was all right with him, I would take his place," the husband said.

Sometimes fate has an odd way of presenting itself, doesn't it? In this case, the beautiful young daughter's future had been protected for her by her parents – who weren't even supposed to be there – while the north wind howled, and the snow piled up outside against the walls of a warm and cozy Italian restaurant in a small Massachusetts town. Keith and I still see the couple at our client dinners and at each annual review. Their daughter and I are friends on Facebook. It occurs to me how many other people there are who, like this couple, are living with situations that cause them worry and concern, and what satisfaction it gave both me and my attorney friend to use our knowledge and expertise to help them find peace of mind.

Parting Advice

It was a bright and sunny weekend, and I was driving home from the beach with my wonderful wife and our three fantastic kids. The weather was superb, the air smelled sweet and everything just seemed right. At least for the present time, all of my past experiences, hard work and over-reaching optimism seemed to be paying off. Life, as the T-shirts say, was good. I wasn't worried about work nor was I stressing about the mortgage. Things just seemed perfect. Then a song came on the radio that brought me back to the summer of 1998. The name of the song was "Sunscreen," and it was based on an article that appeared in the Chicago Tribune a year earlier by Mary Schmich.

The lyrics were bits of advice read by some Australian voice talent and put to a haunting melody. The urban myth is that the lyrics were penned by famed author Kurt Vonnegut for a commencement speech at the Massachusetts Institute of Technology. But that isn't true. As it happens, the sunscreen speech was actually a column written by Chicago Tribune columnist Mary Schmich. Back in 1998, I remember hearing this song and finding the advice not only useful, but as brilliantly plain as it was profound. Here is "the speech."

Wear Sunscreen

By Mary Schmich of the Chicago Tribune

Ladies and gentlemen of the class of '98: Wear sunscreen.

If I could offer you only one tip for the future, sunscreen would be it. The long-term benefits of sunscreen have been proved by scientists whereas the rest of my advice has no basis more reliable than my own meandering experience. I will dispense this advice now.

Enjoy the power and beauty of your youth. Oh, never mind. You will not understand the power and beauty of your youth until they've faded. But trust me, in 20 years, you'll look back at photos of yourself and recall in a way you can't grasp now how much possibility lay before you and how fabulous you really looked. You are not as fat as you imagine.

Don't worry about the future. Or worry, but know that worrying is as effective as trying to solve an algebra equation by chewing bubble gum. The real troubles in your life are apt to be things that never crossed your worried mind, the kind that blind side you at 4 p.m. on some idle Tuesday.

Do one thing every day that scares you.

Sing.

Don't be reckless with other people's hearts. Don't put up with people who are reckless with yours.

Floss.

Don't waste your time on jealousy. Sometimes you're ahead, sometimes you're behind. The race is long and, in the end, it's only with yourself.

Remember compliments you receive. Forget the insults. If you succeed in doing this, tell me how.

Keep your old love letters. Throw away your old bank statements.

Stretch.

Don't feel guilty if you don't know what you want to do with your life. The most interesting people I know didn't know at 22 what they wanted to do with their lives. Some of the most interesting 40-year-olds I know still don't.

Get plenty of calcium.

Be kind to your knees. You'll miss them when they're gone.

Maybe you'll marry, maybe you won't. Maybe you'll have children, maybe you won't. Maybe you'll divorce at 40, maybe you'll dance the funky chicken on your 75th wedding anniversary. Whatever you do, don't congratulate yourself too much, or berate yourself either. Your choices are half chance. So are everybody else's.

Enjoy your body. Use it every way you can. Don't be afraid of it or of what other people think of it. It's the greatest instrument you'll ever own.

Dance, even if you have nowhere to do it but your living room.

Read the directions, even if you don't follow them.

Do not read beauty magazines. They will only make you feel ugly.

Get to know your parents. You never know when they'll be gone for good.

Be nice to your siblings. They're your best link to your past and the people most likely to stick with you in the future.

Understand that friends come and go, but with a precious few you should hold on. Work hard to bridge the gaps in geography and lifestyle, because the older you get, the more you need the people who knew you when you were young.

Live in New York City once, but leave before it makes you hard.

Live in Northern California once, but leave before it makes you soft.

Travel.

Accept certain inalienable truths: Prices will rise. Politicians will philander. You, too, will get old. And when you do, you'll fantasize that when you were young, prices were reasonable, politicians were noble, and children respected their elders.

Respect your elders.

Don't expect anyone else to support you. Maybe you have a trust fund. Maybe you'll have a wealthy spouse. But you never know when either one might run out.

Don't mess too much with your hair or by the time you're 40 it will look 85.

Be careful whose advice you buy, but be patient with those who supply it. Advice is a form of nostalgia. Dispensing it is a way of fishing the past from the disposal, wiping it off, painting over the ugly parts and recycling it for more than it's worth.

But trust me on the sunscreen.

    I bought the little coffee table book that had the words to this column artistically laid out, and I have done my best to follow most of Mary Schmich's advice. I am not saying my life is perfect. It isn't. I am not saying my life is better than that of anyone else. It isn't. I just hope I can look internally and be at peace with my own choices, my own successes and my own failures. What so many people get caught up doing that contributes to their own failures is competing with others rather than themselves. I love the line: "Don't waste your time on jealousy; sometimes you're ahead, sometimes you're behind…the race is long, and in the end, it's only with yourself."

    As a matter of fact, I like to think that one of the best lines in the whole piece is when the author acknowledges that people will choose to either follow or ignore her advice. Everyone has access to the same information. It's what we do with it that makes the difference on how things turn out. In this day and age, the financial advice we dispense should be given along with advice for the soul. That might sound intrusive and unnecessary, but, in the long run, it is all worth it. Money is only as useful and beneficial as the life for which it is set aside to provide. The mistakes and successes you make in how you plan for that life will all stem from something in this song.

    Trust me.

    Wear sunscreen.

After Thought

"Simplicity, patience, compassion.
These three are your greatest treasures.
Simple in actions and thoughts, you return to the source of being.
Patient with both friends and enemies,
you accord with the way things are.
Compassionate toward yourself,
you reconcile all beings in the world."

— Lao Tzu, Tao Te Ching

www.ingramcontent.com/pod-product-compliance
Lightning Source LLC
Chambersburg PA
CBHW071013200526
45171CB00007B/123